"At some stage in their lives, children and adolescents who have an Autism Spectrum Disorder will experience grief but there is remarkably little literature on this emotion for parents, professionals, and those with ASD. Now we have a practical, informative, and sensitive workbook that will encourage the constructive expression of grief. I know this book will be greatly valued by families and those who support them through the grief process."

— *Tony Attwood, Clinical Psychologist, Minds & Hearts Clinic, Brisbane, Australia, and author of* The Complete Guide to Asperger's Syndrome

"Karla Helbert's *Finding Your Own Way to Grieve* fills a gaping need. Her sensitive book will be a godsend to parents, teachers, and therapists supporting a child on the autism spectrum, offering both valuable information and useful exercises that will help that child cope with grief and loss."

— *Kenneth J. Doka, PhD, Professor, The College of New Rochelle, and Senior Consultant, The Hospice Foundation of America*

"Many people on the autism spectrum have a difficult time when an important person in their life dies. This book will help children on the spectrum handle grieving. They can learn that grieving and death are normal parts of life."

— *Temple Grandin, author of* Thinking in Pictures

"Very few books dare to enter or approach human suffering and grief the way that Ms. Helbert's does. With open-hearted compassion and tenderness, she provides much needed guidance to help children with autism who are enduring grief and loss. The book is infused with wisdom and explores grief through discussion topics, exercises, and practical aid which will surely last many children a lifetime. I would recommend it highly for adults and children, professionals, and families, and across cultures."

— *Joanne Cacciatore, PhD, Assistant Professor, Arizona State University and Founder, MISS Foundation*

"Talking about the uncertainties of death is tough for anyone and it is especially so for those of us on the spectrum. Helbert recognizes that our minds crave certainty and absolutism, and that the muddy, murky journey of losing someone close is more than just sad, for us it's an utter betrayal of a promised future. This book offers family members and practitioners concrete, logical methods for walking a young person with Asperger's or autism through the grieving process, and reiterates faithfully that ALL feelings and reactions — no matter how 'different' they are from neurotypical expectations — are alright. In living through a death, as making it through this life, there is no place for the word 'normal'."

— *Jennifer Cook O'Toole, author of* Asperkids: An Insider's Guide to Loving, Understanding and Teaching Children with Asperger Syndrome *and* The Asperkid's (Secret) Book of Social Rules: The Handbook of Not-So-Obvious Social Guidelines for Tweens and Teens with Asperger Syndrome

"Karla Helbert's book is a gem! Her style of writing is simple yet expressive, and will enable individuals with an Autism Spectrum Disorder to finally have a resource to lead them through their grief. As professionals, we need this book to help enrich our support of all individuals grieving the death of a loved one. She gives us the language to explain death through a beautiful story, shares with us journal prompts and checklists to help individuals understand their feelings, and provides unique and meaningful art activities for our clients to remember their loved one. This resource will be a true gift to families, individuals with an Autism Spectrum Disorder, and clinicians everywhere!"

— *Allyson England Drake, Founder and Executive Director, Full Circle Grief Center*

"All of us have to come to grips with loss in our lives. Finally there is a book that will help those with ASD understand one of the greatest mysteries of living. This book is tender, compassionate, and an incredible resource for anyone who cares about and for persons with ASD. It should be on everyone's bookshelf."

— *Carol M. Schall, PhD, Assistant Professor, Director of Training and Technical Assistance and the Autism Center of Excellence, and Director of Virginia Autism Resource Center, Virginia Commonwealth University*

"Helbert's book is saturated with information and activities for helping children understand death and the process of grieving. It is an invaluable resource whether you work with children on the autism spectrum or not. Packed full of creative and expressive projects, I will be using this book over and over in my practice. Thank you, Karla, for creating this much needed resource!"

— *Bonnie Thomas, LCSW, author of* Creative Expression Activities for Teens: Exploring Identity Through Art, Craft and Journaling and Creative Coping Skills for Children: Emotional Support Through Arts and Crafts Activities

"Children with autism will experience loss, whether through the death of a beloved pet, a relative, or a friend. This book addresses issues unique to children or adolescents with autism experiencing loss and is full of practical guidance, resources, and activities for parents or practitioners supporting a child or adolescent with Autism Spectrum Disorder through the grief process. I highly recommend it!"

—*Bradford Hulcher, parent of a son with ASD and Executive Director of the Autism Society, Central VA*

Finding Your Own Way to Grieve

of related interest

Children Also Grieve
Talking about Death and Healing
Linda Goldman
ISBN 978 1 84310 808 5
eISBN 978 1 84642 471 7

Grandad's Ashes
Walter Smith
ISBN 978 1 84310 517 6
eISBN 978 1 84642 605 6

Great Answers to Difficult Questions about Death
What Children Need to Know
Linda Goldman
ISBN 978 1 84905 805 6
eISBN 978 1 84642 957 6

Autism and Loss
Rachel Forrester-Jones and Sarah Broadhurst
ISBN 978 1 84310 433 9
eISBN 978 1 84642 715 2

Grief in Children
A Handbook for Adults
2nd edition
Atle Dyregrov
Foreword by Professor William Yule
ISBN 978 1 84310 612 8
eISBN 978 1 84642 781 7

Finding Your Own Way to Grieve

A Creative Activity Workbook for Kids and Teens on the Autism Spectrum

KARLA HELBERT

Jessica Kingsley *Publishers*
London and Philadelphia

The Toro Nagashi activity, on pp. 121–29, was gratefully adapted from Dick Blick Art Materials® Japanese Floating Lanterns Lesson.
Figure 4.1, on p. 66, has been reproduced with kind permission from Ashley Morris.
Figure 8.2, on p. 108, has been printed with kind permission from Bentley Mescall.

First published in 2013
by Jessica Kingsley Publishers
73 Collier Street
London N1 9BE, UK
and
400 Market Street, Suite 400
Philadelphia, PA 19106, USA

www.jkp.com

Library of Congress Cataloging in Publication Data
A CIP catalog record for this book is available from the Library of Congress

British Library Cataloguing in Publication Data
Helbert, Karla.
  Finding your own way to grieve : a creative activity workbook for kids and teens on the autism spectrum / Karla Helbert.
    p. cm.
  ISBN 978-1-84905-922-0 (alk. paper)
  1. Grief in children. 2. Grief in adolescence. 3. Autistic children. 4. Autistic youth. I. Title.
  BF723.G75H336 2013
  155.9'370874--dc23
                              2012035689

ISBN 978 1 84905 922 0
eISBN 978 0 85700 693 6

Printed and bound by CPI Group (UK) Ltd, Croydon, CR0 4YY

This book is dedicated to Jamie Fueglein, my eternally loving, long-suffering, and unfailingly supportive partner, husband and friend.

To our brilliant, bright, and beautiful daughter Lula Frances Helbert Fueglein, who came trailing clouds of joy.

And always to the life and memory of our precious son Thelonius Luther Helbert Fueglein, known to so many as Theo. You are forever loved and missed more than mere words can convey.

Contents

Acknowledgements

This book would not have been possible without a great deal of help and support from innumerable people. I am unable to mention every person whose help and presence in my life, education, and career has contributed not only to the conception, writing, and completion of this project, but to who I am as a person. That would take a whole book in itself. Since I have this platform, however, I would like to take a moment to mention some of those to whom it is possible to give specific mention. First, I want to thank my husband Jamie Fueglein, who has been a pillar of support to me, not only throughout completion of this book, but in my life overall. Meeting you was a Midsummer Night's Dream come true. Thank you for your love and your patience. His awesome editing talents also contributed greatly to the finished text.

The support and love of my parents has always been a constant for which I am eternally grateful. Thank you both. To my extended family and my friends, those who have been there for us through the darkest of days, before and after, for your deep love, your heartfelt support, your big shoulders and your listening ears, thank you. I could never ask for more supportive, loving people in my life. I am so lucky to have you.

I would never have had cause to write this particular book without those who were instrumental in helping me become who I am as a therapist. I wish to thank Grafton School, Inc. for existing. I am grateful for the amazing people I worked with and learned from during my years there, and most of all for my clients, who taught me that "autism" is a word that means we may be different, but we are also the same. The children, teenagers and adults I worked with early on in my career shaped who I am today and, most important of all, helped me to see the world in a different and better way. I will always be grateful for my experiences with you.

I am grateful to my bright and talented clients, Ashley Morris and Bentley Mescall, who contributed their artwork to this book. It is a privilege to know you both. Thank you for allowing me to be part of your journey and for sharing this part of yourselves with others.

Thank you to Dick Blick Art Materials® for generous permission to use the beautiful Japanese lantern lesson plans. It's one of my favorite projects in the book.

Thank you to Jessica Kingsley Publishers for taking this book on and helping to fill a need where there is a great one to be filled.

Were it not for my own grief journey, this book would not exist. I will never be grateful for the absence of my child in my life. His not being here hurts every day. No matter how it's framed up, I refuse to be grateful for my grief, but I am so grateful for those who have been there from the beginning and for those whom I found along the way. To other bereaved parents, no one knows like you know. I wish things were different for us all, but I am ever grateful for your unmatched understanding.

This list of acknowledgements would be sorely incomplete without mention of my son Theo. Without the fact of the illness that took his life, and which changed me and my family forever, I know I would never have written this book. Since his death, I have an intimate understanding of what Alice meant when she came upon the Caterpillar in Wonderland and he asked, "Who are you?" Alice replied, "I hardly know, sir. I know who I was, but I think I must've changed." Yes. Grief changes us, that surely must be acknowledged, but it doesn't have to stop us from living our lives wholeheartedly, and it can never, ever stop love.

Love is stronger than death.

Letter to the Reader

Dear Reader,

If you are reading this book because someone you love died, I am very sorry that this person has died and that you are hurting. Often, other people might tell you that they are sorry when someone you love has died. You may already have heard other people say this to you. This is not because they feel responsible, but because they feel **sorrow** that this person died and that you are going through such a difficult time in your life. Sometimes, people say they are sorry because they believe they understand some of what you may be **feeling** and they wish that you were not feeling that way. This is because, at some point in life, almost everyone will experience the **death** of someone they love. When we can understand some of what another person may be feeling because we have had a similar experience, we call it having **sympathy**. Typically, when people feel sympathy, they say that they are sorry.

I can have sympathy and understand how much it hurts when someone you love dies because someone I love died too. My son Theo died of a brain tumor on February 20th 2006. A brain tumor is a kind of **cancer** that happens in the brain. Sometimes brain tumors and other kinds of cancer can be cured. The kind my son Theo had could not be cured.

Grief is the word for how we feel when someone we love dies. There are times when I still feel the feelings of grief. When we feel grief, we can say we are grieving. When people we love die, we grieve. Grieving is **normal** and **natural**.

Sometimes, other people can have an idea of how you might be feeling, but everyone experiences the death of a person they love differently.

Grief is very **individual** and **unique** to each person. People have many different feelings when someone they love dies. You may feel sad, angry, confused, upset, lonely, lost, frustrated, or many other feelings. All of the feelings you are experiencing are part of your grief. Your feelings may be strong feelings. Sometimes they may seem too big to handle by yourself. At other times, your feelings may seem soft and small. Still other times, you may feel a mixture of big and small feelings. There may be times when you feel better for a little while and then you feel sad, lonely, angry, confused, frustrated, or upset, all over again. It's okay to feel all of those things, and many more kinds of feelings as well.

Grieving is normal and natural. Everyone grieves at some point in his or her life. Everyone experiences the loss of people, pets, relationships, or very special or important things. It is normal and natural to have feelings of grief when we lose those people, pets, and things that we love which are important parts of our lives. It is normal and natural to feel all kinds of different feelings when you are grieving, and to feel better (or worse) on some days than others. It is normal and natural for your feelings to change when you are grieving.

It is important to know that there is not anything wrong with you. You are grieving. Grief is not a sickness or an illness. Grief is a normal and natural response people have when someone we love dies. It is also important to know that there is no way to know how short or long each person's grief may last. Sometimes it can be very hard not knowing how long you will feel sad or hurt inside. Grieving can sometimes take a long time and this is okay. Grief is not easy, but you can be okay. This book is all about understanding more about your feelings and finding ways to help yourself feel better.

The first chapter of this book is a very short story about death. I originally wrote the story for a boy named Brian. I worked with him as his **therapist**. At the time I wrote the story, he was very sad and confused about the deaths of two people he loved very much. The story seemed to help him understand death and his feelings a little better. Later on, I found that the story helped many different people, children, teenagers, and grown-ups. People with and without **Autism Spectrum Disorder (ASD)**. The story is written in a way that uses clear words to describe death, and many of the different feelings we experience after someone we love dies. This kind of writing and description can be helpful for everyone who is grieving the death of someone they love. Chapter 1 of this book is the original story I wrote for Brian.

The rest of the chapters in the book are based on the short story in Chapter 1. Each of the chapters repeats small sections of the original story and discusses different topics having to do with death, grief, or other feelings you may be experiencing. Each chapter includes activities and suggestions that may help you, or others you know who are grieving. Some of these helpful things involve drawing, painting, or writing. Some are about making things, looking at things, or thinking about things. Some are about moving your body, talking, or playing. I hope that you'll find some things that can help you feel better when you are experiencing the difficult feelings involved with grieving.

There is a glossary at the back of the book to help with the definitions of words that might be new to you. Words that you see in boldface type are in the glossary. **Boldface type looks like this**. Also at the back of the book is a list of **resources**. The resources section includes places, books, people, websites, or organizations that you, or other people you know who are grieving, may choose to seek out and use to find more help, or to increase your knowledge about death, dying, or grief. Many of the resources will also suggest things you can do to help yourself feel better when you are grieving.

Ask an adult to help you with getting a personal notebook or **journal** to write and draw in as you do the different activities in the book. You might choose to decorate the cover of your notebook or journal, or you may choose to keep it plain. You can write, draw, attach, glue or paste anything you choose into your personal notebook or journal. These things might include your private thoughts, dreams, goals, lists, photos, drawings, old gum wrappers, interesting pieces of paper, a leaf you find at the park, whatever you choose. It will be your personal book. You might want to keep it nearby, or carry it with you, in case you feel like writing or drawing or gluing something on the pages. You can also write and draw and glue things directly onto the pages of this book if you choose to. Most of the time it is not okay to write, draw, or glue things onto the pages of a book, but as the author, I give you my personal permission to write, draw, glue or paste things into this one if you choose to do so. There are work pages and other special pages included just for writing, drawing, and gluing things into this book. If you don't want to draw or write in the pages of this book, that is okay too. You can share what you write, draw, or create with someone you trust, or you can choose to keep your writing, drawings, and other activities you work on just for yourself.

Even if you choose not to share, show, or talk about the things you write, draw, make or do, please remember that it is very important to have good **support**. Support means knowing and having people you can trust who will be there to help you when you are sad or when you feel you need help. You might want to talk about your feelings, or you might want to cry with someone, or you might need a hug. Hugs help some people to feel better when they are hurting. Some people do not like hugs, and that's okay too. You can get support and help in all kinds of different ways. Sometimes just having someone sit with you can be a great help. Everyone needs good support when someone they love has died.

I truly hope that this book can help you find ways of feeling better. I hope that you can know that you are not alone, and that other people can understand some of what you may be feeling. This book was written to help you find your own ways of feeling better. You can do all the exercises or suggestions you read about here, some of them, or none at all. Maybe just reading through the book can help you. Whatever you choose, know that your way of feeling better is *your* way. Every person's way—of grieving and of feeling better—is different. Every grieving person shares some similar feelings and experiences, but each person also has his or her own unique and individual experiences. I hope that you find some things in this book to help you on your own individual way of feeling better and moving through the pain of grief. I also hope that the things you find here will help you to find your own unique ways to **honor** and remember the one you love.

With wishes of peace and happiness,
Karla

For Parents, Caregivers, Teachers, and Therapists

Originally, this book's first chapter, "When People Die," was written as a very short story for a young boy on the autism spectrum named Brian. Brian had recently experienced the deaths of both of his grandfathers. The story was written to help him better understand what had happened to his grandfathers, as well as to comprehend his own experience in a more concrete way. In my years of working with children, adolescents, and adults with Autism Spectrum Disorder (as well as other developmental disabilities), I have found that writing things down in a concrete way can help immensely with their understanding and processing of new information. Writing things down also makes the message visual, which is always a plus for anyone, but in particular for those with Autism Spectrum Disorder (ASD). Visual information can be a wonderful tool in helping a child or teenager with ASD adjust to new circumstances or changes, to complete tasks, increase independence, and enhance positive, pro-social behavior. Suggestions for more information and further reading about visual supports for children with ASD can be found in the Resources section of this book.

Since I first used *When People Die* in 2002 to help my young client Brian, that little story has helped many other children with ASD better understand the experience of the death of a loved one. It has also been helpful for children and teens without disabilities. Sharing the story encourages conversation, questions, and togetherness. The story affirms that death is a natural part of life and that grieving is a natural and normal response to death. But the short story alone is limited in scope. We all experience many varied aspects of **grief**—sadness, anger, confusion, loss, anxiety, tears, happiness, laughter, and much more, as we grieve for and remember those we love. Grief manifests as much more than emotional feelings. We all experience grief physically, cognitively, mentally, spiritually. Building on concepts introduced in the short story of Chapter 1, the rest of this book expands on and acknowledges the very many ways grief affects us. It provides different possibilities and methods for your unique child to express and explore the individual ways he or she is personally affected by grief.

For a person with ASD, the myriad facets of grief can be potentially even more confusing and distressing than for a neurotypically functioning individual. For example, sensory perception difficulties may emerge where there were none previously, or existing sensory issues may increase or change. You may notice behavioral changes, subtle or overt. Your child may have feelings, sensations, or experiences that are very different from their usual, but be seemingly unaware of these differences. Symptoms of ASD may increase (e.g., in the form of withdrawal or lessened social interaction, increased focus on obsessions or highly focused interests, increased need for sameness, predictability).They will need your help to stay balanced and healthy. Noticing and being aware of how your child is experiencing and reacting to this major life event is paramount. Through it all, it is important to remember that grief, as distressing as it can be, is a normal and natural response to the death of a loved one, and also that grief is completely individual for us all. It is also important for children to see that their parents and caregivers grieve as well. If you are also grieving, be willing to your let your child know this. By example, and with a willingness to be open to our own grief experiences as natural and normal, we can show our children how to grieve in healthy ways.

This book and its accompanying activities are particularly helpful for children with ASD for many reasons. The clear, concise language can help them approach and better understand the difficult, fairly abstract concepts of death and grief. The exercises and activities throughout help the child explore and be more comfortable with the changes they are experiencing as a result of grief. I recommend that you encourage the child to do the checklists and exploratory exercises throughout the book. These can give valuable information to the child about his or her own experience, and to you about how to better help. The child's answers and responses to those activities can help you know more about the questions they may have as well as how they may be affected on many different levels by their individual experience of grief.

Overall, a child, or any person, with ASD will experience the same range of symptoms of grief as any other person in the same developmental stage of life. Young children may display regressive behavior, acting younger than they are, or exhibit behaviors they had previously "grown out of." They may become more demanding or require more comfort or attention. They may become more fearful, have bad dreams, or fear the death of others. Depending on the child and the manner of death of the person, some children can experience self-blame, or believe that their thoughts may have caused bad things. All younger children, and some older children, can have a hard time understanding the abstract concept of death and its permanence. They can have difficulty, in particular, with the many ways that grown-ups tend to talk about death, with and around them. Children with ASD, including older children and teens, will very likely have an even more difficult time with this particular aspect of the way society talks about death. To help with this, avoid speaking in abstractions or giving confusing responses about the loved one's death. Saying things like, "We lost Grandpa," can be very confusing. The child may think, or ask, "Why can't we find him? Where did he get lost?" Other common phrases such as "She has passed away" or "He's in a better place" require further explanation and clarification for the child. In general, when talking to a child or teen with ASD, be as concrete as possible. Avoid using euphemisms for death and be sure that they understand that the person has died and is not "lost," or simply someplace else. Always tell the truth and be clear. Words and phrases that may seem to make others feel more comfortable about death can create confusion for any child, and especially a child with autism.

Teenagers and "tweens" do not like to be considered children, and don't like to feel different from their peers. Even though a teen with ASD may not behave in the typical teenage manner of his or her peers, he or she most likely will have the teenaged need to be considered as an individual who is trusted, respected and treated as an equal in as many ways as possible. They need to be told the truth, the facts, allowed to ask questions, and to feel supported in expressing thoughts and feelings about their experience.

Here is a list of helpful strategies for everyone to remember when supporting a child or teen with ASD who is grieving:

- Be concrete when speaking to the child about what has happened. Answer questions in as concrete a manner as possible. Avoid euphemisms for death. Use the words "dead," "death," and "died" when speaking of the death.

- Understand that even if they do not speak, they are grieving. Also, remember that not speaking is not the same as not having anything to say.

- Even if they don't speak, or even seem to understand what is going on, operate under the assumption that they are aware, and treat them in this manner.

- Understand that tears, or the lack of tears, are not a measure of how much the child is grieving. It is okay if they do not cry, it is okay if they do cry. Help them to know this.

- Tell them the truth about the death, and about any rituals or traditions, without overcomplicating the message. Give them facts and allow them time and space to process the information as well as ask questions.

- Allow them to make decisions about their own grief process.

- Be as consistent as possible with the child's schedule of activities, including a reliable daily schedule and night time rituals.

- Ensure plenty of nutritious food and pay close attention to their food intake and hydration. It is very common for people to experience changes in diet and appetite when they are grieving. Many children and teens with ASD experience difficulties with food, eating and drinking (as well as the general listening to of various body signals), at the best of times. It is very likely that they will have increased difficulties in these areas when in grief.

- Nearly all people with ASD experience sensory processing difficulties of some kind. Be aware of your child's sensory processing issues and understand that sensory processing difficulties may increase during, or as a result of, grief. New or previously unseen sensory difficulties may emerge during, or as a result of, grief. Look for and notice any changes in sensory perception. Communicate about sensory perception issues or difficulties with the child. Let him or her know that they are safe. Communicate with the child about ways to help resolve sensory difficulties and explore these as best you can. Some ways to help with these changes may mean keeping lights low, avoiding fluorescent lighting, keeping auditory stimulation at a minimum, avoiding crowds, increasing periods of time for exercise or other physical activity, or providing deep pressure (squeezing of large muscle groups, allowing the child to wrap him or herself in blankets or wear clothing that facilitates pressure on muscle groups, bear hugs, etc.), according to the needs of your child. Knowing your child and his or her needs in these areas is key in assisting with sensory difficulties.

- Encourage communication in whatever ways the child communicates best. The checklists and exploratory questions in this book are very helpful for assisting with communication.

- Encourage learning new activities, new ways of creating and finding ways to direct energy, in whatever ways suit the child and his or her individual interests.

- Support the child in finding ways to **mourn** and to remember the person they love who has died in ways that are authentic to the child and her or her personality and abilities.

- Share this list with your child's caregivers and teachers.

- Be patient with your child's individual grief process.

English philosopher George Henry Lewes said, "The only cure for grief is action."[1] Through my own grief journey, and through helping many other people traveling the same road, I have discovered that this is absolutely true. What sorts of actions a grieving person takes is highly individual. Those actions may include art-making, writing, baking, exercising, gardening, creating **rituals** and memorials for the one who has died, or any number of other activities, but whatever the action, it requires purposefulness and mindfulness. The healing actions should be intentional acts of doing or creating something with the purpose of working through your individual grief, as well as those actions which are done to honor and remember your loved one.

I encourage you to use this book with the child who is grieving. Some children and adolescents with ASD, or other pervasive developmental or intellectual disabilities, may need help with reading, gathering materials, or engaging in the various activities. They may need help getting started or help in sharing their experiences or feelings. Some of the activities may appeal strongly to some children, while others may not. Some may enjoy the writing prompts, others may prefer the arts or crafts, and still others, the movement-based activities. Much of the information in this book transcends disability and ability, as well as age or station in life. It can be adapted to the needs of your child and those of yourself or others you may know who are grieving.

Grief, and the actions we choose to help us **mourn** and to express our feelings, are highly individual. It is only in trying different things that we find what works for each of us. Many of the activities can easily translate to group and family activities and rituals. I also suggest that if you are grieving along with the child, you get your own notebook or journal and engage in some of the activities on your own. Additionally, there is a glossary in the back of the book to help in explaining what may be new words or concepts for some readers. The glossary words are set in **boldface type** the first time they appear in the book. Many of the worksheets and other content are available as free downloads for your personal use.

As a family member or a professional, there are many things you can do to help your grieving child. You can be there for the child. You can

---

1   Lewis, G. H. (1846) *The Spanish Drama.* London: Charles Knight & Co, p.42.

talk, read, play, and always be honest with the child about what has happened. You can observe special days, such as the loved one's birthday, and the **anniversary** of the death, and allow the child to participate. Acknowledge the loved one's absence and memory on other special days as appropriate, such as Mother's Day, Father's Day, Grandparents Day, and other holidays. Religious, secular, and national holidays can be painful when those we love are not there to share in the festivities. Help the child share in remembrance activities at holidays and other special times. Encourage the child to be expressive and engage in activities that help him or her work through and understand the difficult feelings and experiences of grief. This book can help you do these things. If you are grieving also, do the same for yourself. Be gentle with the child and be gentle with yourself.

For family members in particular, I hope this book can help you and your family find ways to help yourselves move forward and through the pain and sadness of grief, to learn new ways of living more fully and expressively (even with the painful fact of your loss), to honor your own experience, and to find new and meaningful ways to remember those you love who have died.

For professionals and caregivers, my wish is that this book can assist you in discovering practical and creative ways to help the children and teenagers you serve to manage their experiences of grief and loss. Many professionals who work in grief support may not have particular experience or expertise in supporting those on the autism spectrum. I hope that this book can help you to be better equipped to provide the much needed support when those children and teens come to you or your program for help. For professionals whose expertise is in autism, and not necessarily grief, I hope this book will help you to share more fully in the journeys of those you support when they are in pain. Everyone grieves when someone we love has died. The greatest thing you can give a grieving person is support, love, a non-judgemental listening ear, and the ability to communicate and express his or her feelings and experiences. Your support is so important. Thank you for being there for them when they need you.

In all their memories,

Karla

Some Tips for Success when Doing Crafts, Art or Cooking Projects

1. Prepare your space. Make sure that your workspace is covered with newspaper or a plastic or paper table cloth. If you are cooking, make sure your hands, your preparation and cooking areas are clean.

2. Wear clothing and shoes that you don't mind getting a little messy. But try to relax, you can never completely avoid messes when making things.

3. Wash your hands before beginning your activity. It's always good to start with clean hands. If your hands get messy while making your project (with glue or paint or food), it is good to stop to clean your hands between steps. Wash your hands afterward to remove any paint, glue, or other material you were working with.

4. Follow each step carefully. Each project in this book will turn out as it says. Remember, though, that your finished product does not have to, and should not, look exactly, or even almost, like the pictures in the book. I encourage you to be as creative and expressive as you like in making things that reflect who you are. If you need help reading or following any of the activity steps, ask a grown-up or older teen to help.

5. Be patient. You may need to wait while paint or glue dries, or while something bakes.

6. If the project gives measurements, follow the measurements. Most of the projects allow for changes and creativity, but some require precise measurements (like baking bread).

7. Clean up your mess when you are finished. Store your arts and crafts materials together so that everything you need will be ready the next time you want to create something.

8. Have fun! Even though you may be missing the one you love who died, creating and making things is still fun. It's okay to have fun, even when we are feeling sad inside.

Chapter 1

When People Die

(A very short story about death)

Everything that lives must die.

Flowers die, trees die, animals die, and people die too.

Dying is a part of life.

People die when their bodies stop working.

This means they do not breathe air anymore.

Their heart stops beating and pumping blood through their bodies.

When people are dead, sometimes they look like they are asleep, but they are not asleep.

The body is there, but it does not wake up.

The body does not need to sleep.

It does not feel pain anymore.

It does not feel cold or hot anymore.

It does not need to eat or drink anymore.

When we see the body, it seems like the person we know is not in that body anymore.

Some people say that the real person we know is not the body, but the "spirit."

Our bodies hold our spirits while we are alive.

When our bodies die, our spirits leave our bodies just like we can leave a house.

The spirit leaves when the body stops working.

The spirit goes somewhere else.

We don't know for sure where the spirit goes.

Some people believe that the spirits of people who die go to heaven.

This is a nice place to think of.

It is okay to think of the people we love being in heaven after their bodies are dead.

Heaven would be a very happy and safe place to be.

It is okay to feel sad or even angry when someone we love dies.

When someone we love dies, we miss them.

It is okay to miss the people we love.

When we feel sad or angry we can talk about how we feel with friends, family or others we trust.

We can always remember the people we love who have died.

We can tell other people about them.

We can talk about the fun things we did, the games we played, or the places we visited.

We can look at pictures of them, and pictures of us together when they were alive.

We will always miss them.

We will always love them.

It's okay to be sad sometimes.

It's okay to cry sometimes.

But we can be happy too, and it's okay!

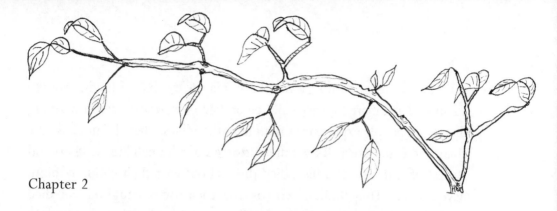

Chapter 2

Dying is a Part of Life

Everything that lives must die.
Flowers die, trees die, animals die, and people die too.
Dying is a part of life.

Every living thing is different, but every living thing must someday die. Dying is a natural part of life. Usually, people do not die until they have lived many years. All animals and people have a **lifespan**, which is the expected, average time that a particular species of any animal, including humans, will live. The lifespan of a person is usually about 80 years. This is only an average. Some people may die much earlier or much later. The oldest known person at the time of this writing lived 122 years and 164 days. Sometimes people and animals die before a natural lifespan is completed, due to illness or injuries that cannot be cured or healed. People of all ages can die because of illness, injury, disease or accidents. This can happen at any age. Sometimes children die. Sometimes little babies can die. Babies can die at birth, or sometimes even before they are born. It is rarer for babies and older children to die than for adults and older people, but it does happen.

When babies and children die, it can seem even sadder than when an older person dies. This is because people usually feel that it seems very unfair that a little baby, a child, or a very young person will not get a chance to live what people call a "full life." This means that they did not get a chance to grow up, go to school, play, learn, have friends, grow to adulthood, get married, have children of their own, or experience anything that living people experience throughout their lives. They did not have the chance to experience all the different stages of a human life. Mothers and fathers of children who have died think about who their children might have become. They think of who or what their son or daughter who died might have grown up to be, or do. They wonder what their child might have looked like as an older child, a teenager, as a grown-up. They wonder what choices their child might have made. They think about missing out on their children's lives. These thoughts can make parents very, very sad. These sad thoughts and feelings never really go away.

If you have a brother or sister who has died, you may notice that your mother or father, or other people in your family, are very sad, for a very long time. Sometimes, even after your parents seem to feel better, they can still be very, very sad at times. One of the best things to help a mother or a father whose child has died is to let them know that others think about and remember that child too. You can be helpful by letting them know you care about them, and about the child who died, even when you are grieving too. This is called being a good support person. Remember that you won't make them feel sadder by talking about their child who has died. They like knowing that others are thinking of, and missing, that child too.

It is impossible to predict when someone will die. Sometimes we can know that a person is dying if he or she has an illness or an injury that cannot be treated or made better. The person's doctor can tell the family that there are no more treatments that can make the person better, and that the person will die. Sometimes when this happens, an organization called a **hospice** can help the dying person to make sure that the person is comfortable, that they are not in pain, and that their death is as peaceful and as painless as possible. They can also help family members through the dying person's illness and death. Even with hospice support, we still cannot know exactly when a person will die. Death is often called a "mystery" because it is one of the things in life that no one can know everything about, and cannot be fully explained. We cannot predict the exact time when death will happen. We cannot know exactly what each person's death will be like. We cannot know exactly what happens to each person after the person has died.

When someone you love dies, many things can be very difficult. Your feelings can be hard to understand. It can be hard to put questions or concerns you may have into words. Sometimes it can be hard to know who might be able to answer questions, or who it is okay to talk to. Sometimes people do not like to talk about, or think about, death. Some people feel afraid, worried, or uncomfortable when they talk about, or think about, death. They may also feel afraid, worried or uncomfortable when they hear others talking about death. It is important to remember that it is okay to feel afraid, worried, uncomfortable, or even confused, especially when someone you love has died. You may find that the more you talk about how you feel, the more you write down your feelings, the more you do art and create things, like drawings, paintings, sculptures, or other kinds of creations surrounding your questions and feelings about grief, the less worried, afraid, and confused you may become.

Asking Questions

Spend some time talking to someone you trust about death. Write down questions you have about death in your journal, or use the space below. If you have difficulty writing, you can ask a trusted person to write them down for you as you **dictate**. They may be general, broad questions about death, or very specific questions about the death of someone you know or love. Sometimes just being able to ask or write down the questions can help, even if you don't know the answers. You can share your questions with someone you trust who may be able to help you find some answers. If some of your questions can be answered, you may feel a bit better.

Here are some questions that you might ask about death:

- What are your thoughts and feelings about death?

- Did you ever spend any time thinking about death before this important person in your life died?

- Did you ever see a dead animal or bird on the side of the road?

- Did you ever notice the differences in plants that were blooming and growing, and those that were withered, brown, and without life?

- Have you known or heard of other people who died? How old were you then? What did you think or know about the death?

- Did you ever ask questions about death?

- Did you know that all living things must one day die?

- Why do you think living things must die?

You may want to stop here for a moment, get your notebook or journal, and write down your own personal answers to some or all of the above questions. If you are sharing this book with a trusted person, you may wish to stop and talk about your thoughts on some or all of the above questions. If you like, you can write down questions and thoughts in this book. You can use the above questions or you can come up with questions of your own. You don't have to know the answers to the questions, you can just think about the questions, or you can write down things that the questions might cause you to think about. Sometimes, certain questions we have may cause us to think of other questions. Some questions we may not always have answers for. This is okay. It is important to continue to ask questions and to think about things that we are curious about. Asking and thinking about questions helps us to learn and to be more **comfortable** with difficult topics, like grief and death.

My Questions About Death and Grief

Question 1: . . . .

. . . .

My own personal thoughts about the above question: . . . .

. . . .

. . . .

Question 2: . . . .

. . . .

My own personal thoughts about the above question: . . . .

. . . .

. . . .

Question 3: . . . .

. . . .

My own personal thoughts about the above question: . . . .

. . . .

. . . .

Question 4: . . . .

. . . .

My own personal thoughts about the above question: . . . .

. . . .

. . . .

Question 5: . . . .

. . . .

My own personal thoughts about the above question: . . . .

. . . .

. . . .

Question 6: . . . .

. . . .

My own personal thoughts about the above question: . . . .

. . . .

. . . .

Use your own journal or notebook if you need extra space or have more than six questions.

It is important to remember that sometimes, people are not able to have all the answers we want right away. Sometimes, we may not like the answers we find. Sometimes, we may never find any answers at all to some of our questions. When we cannot find answers to our questions, or when we do not like, or do not understand the answers, this can cause even more difficult feelings. When this happens, we can try to find other ways to help us **cope** with our feelings. Some other ways may be talking with people we trust, or doing other things like drawing, writing, painting, or making things. Sometimes doing a physical activity, like walking, running, or dancing, may also help us cope with our feelings.

When someone you love dies, it is a very hard time in your life. When someone you love dies, it is a time of great change. Many people with ASD have a very difficult time when things change. The death of someone you love can be one of the biggest changes you will ever experience. The closer you are to the person who has died, the more deeply your grief will affect you. Also, the closer you are to the person who has died, the bigger and more difficult are the changes. It is important for you to know that when someone you love dies, it can feel like a time of great **chaos**. "Chaos" means disorder, confusion, and uncertainty. In grief, it can be very difficult to know how you will feel from one moment to the next.

This not knowing how you will feel can be scary. It is also very normal to feel that way when someone you love dies. It is also normal to not feel that way. It is important to know that if you are feeling that way, chaotic, disordered, confused, uncertain, and scared, these are normal feelings during grief. It is also good to know that you will not feel that way all the time. You will not feel that way forever.

If you are the type of person who needs to have a very dependable schedule, and who needs to know what will happen to you throughout your day, this aspect of grief may be especially hard for you. There are many intelligent people who agree that one of the most chaotic and uncertain times during a human life can be when we are grieving the death of a loved one. We cannot predict how we may feel from one moment to the next. This can be very hard. Your parents or caregivers may also be grieving and experiencing these kinds of chaotic feelings. The changes they are going through may be very hard for you as well. Those people who have been dependable in your life may seem and act very different while they are grieving.

It would be helpful to talk about changes with your parents or caregivers. Those people can talk with you about how things may change, or they can write or type them out for you. If you are a person who uses a schedule or a personal planner, it may be helpful to make changes in your schedule or personal planner with someone who can help you understand and work through the changes. Changes might include people you will spend time with, places that you will go, things that you will be doing.

If you are not a person who has used a schedule or a personal planner in the past, you may find that writing down or having someone else help you write down your schedule and what you will be doing can help you feel calmer and more at ease.

Changes in my Life

If you like, you can use the space below to make some notes and share your experiences about how things have been different since your loved one died. You can also use the space to write down things that you need to help you feel better, and the things you really miss about the way your life was before your loved one died.

You may also choose to use the worksheet area to help express how you are feeling. Remember that it may feel very difficult, but you can learn ways to help you cope with your grief, as well as ways to help you remember the one you love who died.

If you need extra space for any of the following exercises, you can use the blank pages in the back of the book, or write in your own personal notebook or journal.

These are some of the ways things have changed since _____ *died:*

1. . . . .

   . . . .

2. . . . .

   . . . .

3. . . . .

   . . . .

4. . . . .

   . . . .

5. . . . .

   . . . .

I really miss the following things about the way my life was before _____ *died:*

1. . . . .

   . . . .

2. . . . .

   . . . .

3. ·

· ·

4. ·

· ·

5. ·

· ·

These are some of the things that I think
might help me to feel better:

1. ·

· ·

2. ·

· ·

3. ·

· ·

4. ·

· ·

5. ·

· ·

Thinking About My Feelings

It can be very helpful to understand more about your own feelings and experiences. This can be true at any time in your life. Having a greater understanding of your feelings can help you be a more satisfied person. When we are grieving, many of our feelings are very difficult to understand. The following exercise can help you to better identify your own feelings and experiences. It can also help you to be able to share them with others. Circle or check off (tick) any of the following things that are true for you since your loved one died.

1. ☐ My feelings have been overwhelming.

2. ☐ I have not felt very strong feelings.

3. ☐ I have felt confused.

4. ☐ I have been worried.

5. ☐ I have felt sad.

6. ☐ I have felt frustrated.

7. ☐ I have felt angry.

8. ☐ I have felt afraid.

9. ☐ I have had difficulty concentrating or thinking.

10. ☐ I have been in physical pain.

11. ☐ I have felt guilty.

12. ☐ I have felt tired.

13. ☐ I have felt happy.

14. ☐ I have felt calm.

15. ☐ I am not able to keep track of things in my life.

16. ☐ I do not like thinking about the person I love who has died.

17. ☐ I want to think about the person I love who has died.

18. ☐ I sometimes forget that the person I loved has died.

19. ☐ I have had problems sleeping.

✓   20. ☐ I have had problems with eating.

21. ☐ I have had problems with seeing, hearing, smelling, or tasting things.

22. ☐ I have had problems with how my clothes fit, how things feel against my skin.

23. ☐ I have had other kinds of physical problems or feelings that I can't explain.

24. ☐ I want to talk about how I feel, but do not know how.

25. ☐ I have not felt or experienced any of the above.

26. ☐ I do not know how I feel.

27. ☐ I want to talk more about some of the things I checked above.

28. ☐ There are things I feel or have experienced that are not on this checklist.

29. ☐ There are things that I want to know about _____'s death.

30. ☐ I do not want to know any more information about _____'s death.

31. ☐ I don't know how things will change since _____ died.

32. ☐ I am worried about how things will change since _____ died.

33. ☐ I want someone to talk with me about the changes in my life that may happen now.

34. ☐ I know who I would like to talk with.

35. ☐ I would like to talk to _____.

It is okay if you checked off many of the things on the list above, and it is also okay if you checked only a few, or none. If you would

✓

like to know more about, or talk more about, any of the things in the above list, you can circle the numbers of those things above, or write them below. If you want to talk about some feelings or experiences or concerns that are not in the checklist, you can also write those below.

I want to know or talk more about the
following items on the feeling checklist:

. . . .

. . . .

. . . .

. . . .

I want to know something about a feeling
or an experience that is not on the checklist
above. That feeling or experience is:

. . . .

. . . .

. . . .

. . . .

The information you have communicated is very important and should be shared with someone you trust. Please do let someone know about this information. Feel free to talk about or write about these things as well. Sharing how you feel with your support people can be very helpful when you are grieving. Those people can help you feel more calm and can help you to know that you are not alone in your grief. It is also important to know that all the feelings and experiences on the checklist above are normal experiences and feelings when we are grieving a person we love who has died.

   You can also use your journal or the blank pages at the end of the book to draw or write something about what you are feeling.

✓

Chapter 3

People Die When Their Bodies Stop Working

People die when their bodies stop working.
This means they do not breathe air anymore.
Their heart stops beating and pumping blood through their bodies.

Our hearts are muscles that pump blood through our bodies when we are alive. This is the technical, scientific function of our hearts. There are also many expressions in the English language involving the heart as it relates to our **emotions**. The fact that people seem to experience many different kinds of strong feelings in the heart area may be the reason for the existence of so many expressions about the heart.

When sad or hurt, someone might say that his or her heart is "broken." This is because sometimes when we are so sad, as we are after someone we love has died, we can feel the hurt right in the middle of our chests, just where our hearts are located in our physical bodies. We often feel love in this part of our bodies too. We may say that we are "brokenhearted" to describe how we feel when we are sad or hurt emotionally. Sometimes people say someone is "heartsick" when something very sad or disappointing has happened. Sometimes you may feel as though your heart actually or literally "sinks" when you are disappointed, or that your heart is "heavy" when you are sad. Some heart sayings compare conscience (knowing right from wrong) with a "knowing" in your heart if a bad or a wrong decision has been made. They believe that you can "know in your heart" what may be the right thing to do in a confusing or difficult situation. We may say (and even feel) that we have a "full" heart when we are feeling more than one emotion at once, such as **gratitude** and love. People often say they have a "joyful heart" when they are feeling very happy and full of joy. When two people decide to have a very personal and truthful conversation, they may call this having a "heart-to-heart" talk. The heart has a very important role in feelings and when we describe human emotions.

As in the "full heart" example described above, our hearts really can seem to hold many different feelings at once. This can be especially true when someone we love has died. Sometimes, all the different feelings you may be feeling can be confusing. It is important to remember that it is absolutely okay to have a lot of different feelings, even at the same time. The Color Your Heart exercise below can help you to sort through and think about the different kinds of feelings you are having right now.

Color Your Heart

To begin, choose as many colors as you like from a box of crayons, markers, colored pencils or pastels. Decide that each color you choose will stand for a feeling you are having right now (or in the moment that you are doing this exercise). For example: blue might mean sadness, red could mean anger, yellow could be happiness, like that. Take your time to decide what feelings *you* are having and what colors will represent each of *your* own feelings in the moment. You might decide to choose colors first and then decide which feelings they represent, or you could make a list of all the different feelings you are having and then decide what color best represents each feeling. Do what feels right to you. There is no right way to do this exercise. It is important only to somehow decide what colors you want to assign to your own feelings and then to remember which colors represent which feelings.

To help with this, you can fill in the color key at the bottom of the page to show what colors represent which feelings. On a map, the key uses words or phrases to show what the **symbols** on the map mean. Your colors will be the symbols for your feelings. Your color key will remind you what colors represent which feelings.

When you have decided what colors will be which feelings, and have made your color key, color in your heart to show how much of each feeling your heart is holding right now. Your heart picture might be divided like a pie, filled with stripes, whorls, symbols, shading, designs—or a picture that you create inside the heart outline. When you are finished, you can share your picture of your heart with someone you trust, explaining your colors and feelings, the things you drew, and how it felt to do the activity. You can also write about it in your journal.

You might find it interesting and helpful to do this exercise each week or each month to help you understand how your feelings change over time. You can draw your own heart shape on a piece of paper, or you can use the one here in the book to trace the shape. It is important to remember that our feelings are always changing, especially when we are grieving. This exercise especially can help us to see how our feelings can be different at different times. It can also help us understand how we can have many different feelings at once.

Color my Heart Exercise

My color key:

Color	Feeling
☐	sad
☐	angry
☐	happy
☐	_____
☐	_____
☐	_____
☐	_____
☐	_____

✓

✓

When people are dead, sometimes they look like they are asleep, but they are not asleep.
The body is there, but it does not wake up.
The body does not need to sleep.
It does not feel pain anymore.
It does not feel cold or hot anymore.
It does not need to eat or drink anymore.
When we see the body, it seems like the person we know is not in that body anymore.

If you saw or touched your loved one's body after death, like at the **funeral**, or if you were there in the home or hospital just after he or she died, you probably already know that after death the body feels very different to the touch than it does when it is alive. These differences help us to know that the person we love is no longer feeling the same sensations within their body. We can see that they are not breathing. Their skin feels different to our touch. If we could listen to their chests, we would not hear a heartbeat. We can know that all these things mean that the one we love is not feeling any pain, or hunger, or cold. This is a good thing. We need to know that the people we love who have died are safe, that their bodies are not feeling cold, or hurt, or anything bad. It is good to know this. But knowing this does not mean that we do not feel sad to be without them.

A lot of times when we have strong feelings—good or bad—we feel them in our bodies at different places. Everyone experiences their feelings at different places in the body. You may have heard people say that they have "butterflies in their stomach," a "lump in the throat," or a "heavy" heart. There aren't real butterflies in anyone's stomach, hearts don't really get heavier. We have feelings sometimes that cause sensations in our bodies in those areas, such as where our hearts or our stomachs are located. Thinking about, talking about, and drawing your feelings can help you to know what they are and where you are feeling them in your body. It is good to know where you feel your feelings in your body. Knowing more about how you feel and understanding more about how your body feels things, can help you to be more comfortable with your feelings, even when the feelings are not good ones.

Included in feelings and experiences is the way each person's brain processes sensory information. **Sensory processing** is how your brain and body recognize, interpret, or experience sensory information from all the different senses of the body. These include the five most well known senses: seeing, hearing, touching, tasting, and smelling. There are also four other senses that provide information about how our bodies experience the world. These include how your body perceives temperature and pain, how your body experiences balance and movement, and awareness of your body and its various parts in space. Check the glossary for the definition and more information on sensory processing and the nine senses of the body.

It is important to understand that every person experiences and processes sensory information differently at different times. It is good to learn the different ways that your body experiences and processes different kinds of sensory input. It can be very helpful to know that sometimes difficult experiences (including the death of someone you love) can create stress that might cause changes or differences in sensory perception and processing. You may notice changes in how you see or hear things—colors or patterns may seem brighter and bigger, sounds may seem louder or more difficult to separate. You may notices differences in the ways that your body responds to touch or sensations of pressure.

For a person with ASD, sensory changes can sometimes feel overwhelming. These kinds of changes can feel scary, uncomfortable, distracting, interesting, pleasant, painful, bothersome and many other sensations, depending on each person's experience. Sensory processing difficulties and changes can be a challenge for a person with ASD at any time in life, but the experience of grief may cause more or different sensory changes than are typical for any individual person. The changes may happen very unexpectedly. If you do notice changes in your sensory processing, it can be helpful to try to find ways to communicate about the changes with people you trust. You may want to share this section of the book with someone who knows the kinds of sensory experiences that you typically have, and try to help them know about any changes you might be experiencing. Even if you are not experiencing changes, sharing this information will help others to know that changes in sensory processing *can* happen when someone is grieving or under stress. The next exercise may help you identify the different ways your body may be experiencing feelings and sensations.

Body Map Exercise

Here are two different ways to make a Body Map to help you understand what you are feeling and where you are feeling things in your body. You can ask an adult to help you to get a BIG sheet of paper. A roll of **butcher's paper** or a large roll of craft paper can also work well. You can also unglue and smooth out paper grocery bags, cut the bottoms of the bags away, and then tape together several pieces of the brown paper bags until the surface is large enough for you to lay your whole body down on it. This can work, but sometimes the edges get in the way. A good thing about working with a really big piece of paper is that you can have your own real life-sized body shape to work with and plenty of room to draw lots of feelings onto your Body Map.

If you are using a big piece of paper, you will probably need someone to help you trace the shape of your body onto your large sheet of paper. Use a dark color for your outline so it will show up better. You can always use a pencil first and then trace over your body outline with a marker.

If you don't want to do a life-sized version, or if you don't have a big piece of paper, you can also use a regular piece of drawing paper and draw a shape that looks like a body, just smaller. The small version can sometimes be easier to work with. You can even try the Body Map both ways to see which one works better for you. You can also use the body shape here in this book for your Body Map. Remember that the body outline does not need to look exactly like your real body—it is only a **representation** of your body, not a realistic **portrait** of yourself.

Once you have your body shape outlined on the paper, stop for a few minutes to think about your body and the feelings you notice inside or outside your body. A **feeling** can mean a physical sensation like a tickle or an itch, or pain from a bruise or cut, or tightness in your muscles. A feeling can also mean an emotion, like sadness, joy, or confusion. Both kinds of feelings (physical and emotional) are okay to experience, and both are good to draw onto your body map. You may find that you have more emotional types of feelings in certain places than in others. We tend to feel a lot of emotions in the middle parts of our bodies. Places like the stomach, heart, chest and throat. Try to pay close attention to the feelings you might have in these areas. Sometimes it can be hard to name feelings. If you can't think of a name for what you are feeling, choose colors that remind you of your feelings and draw **images**, shapes, or lines in ways that remind you of those feelings. If you can think of words for your feelings, you can write or draw the words for the feelings. You can use images, symbols, words, or a combination of all those things.

Start from your toes and move up. You can close your eyes to do this if it makes it easier to think about your feelings that way. You can even lie down on your body map to think about your feelings. Think about your toes, your feet, your ankles, your calves, your knees, your thighs. What do you feel in those areas? You may or may not feel much in these areas. You might feel some **tension** in your muscles. You might feel tired or jumpy in your feet and legs. Whatever you are feeling is okay, just notice.

Stop and draw what you feel in your toes, feet, ankles, and legs.

Next, think about your fingers, hands, arms and shoulders. What are you feeling in those places? Again, it's okay to feel strong feelings or not. Just notice what you are feeling in those places.

Stop and draw what you feel in your fingers, hands, arms and shoulders.

Think about your belly, your stomach, your back, your chest, your heart and your neck. Notice what you are feeling in those parts of your body. You might have different feelings in your belly area from those in your heart area. Those feelings might also be different from those you feel in your chest, shoulders, back and neck. This is okay. These are places in our bodies where we tend to hold very strong feelings. You might want to spend a little longer thinking about these areas.

When you are ready, stop and draw onto your Body Map what you feel in your belly, your stomach, your back, your lungs, your chest, your heart and your neck.

Last, think about your head, your face, your eyes, your ears, and the top of your head. Feel what you are feeling in those parts of your body. You might also notice thoughts about what you are doing, or what might be happening in your brain.

Stop and draw what you are feeling in your head, your face, your eyes, and your ears. You can also draw thoughts that might be happening in your brain if you choose.

If you wish, share your drawings with an adult or a trusted friend. It can be very helpful to share this exercise with another person. As you explain what your Body Map tells about your body and what feelings you are showing in your Body Map, it can help you understand your feelings even better. As you share your Body Map, you may notice your feelings getting stronger. This is okay. If you cry, this is also okay. If you do not cry, this is okay too. You may also want to write about your Body Map in a poem, a story or in your journal. It is important to remember that no feeling lasts forever. Our feelings change. This is normal and natural.

Body Map Outline

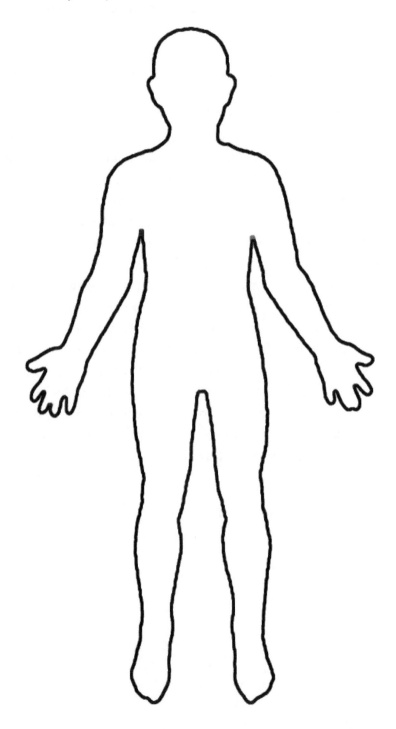

✓

Example of a Body map

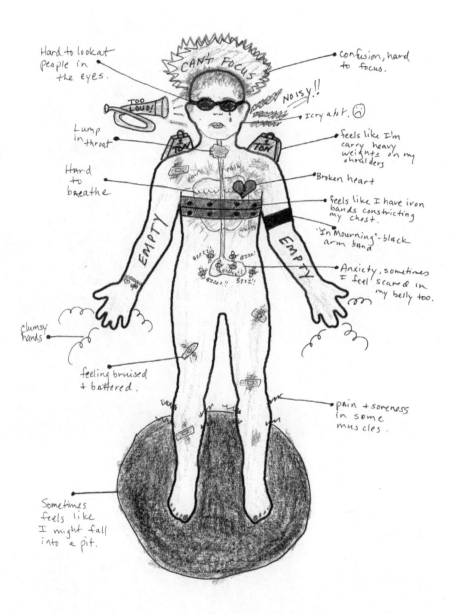

Here is an example of what a Body Map using the blank body figure, provided on the previous page might look like. If you notice, the drawing includes emotional feelings, physical sensations, and sensory experiences. You can feel free to use words or not. Your Body Map should reflect you and your experiences in your own body, in your own way.

Chapter 4

Heaven Would Be a Very Happy and Safe Place to Be

Some people say that the real person we know is not the body, but the "spirit."
Our bodies hold our spirits while we are alive.
When our bodies die, our spirits leave our bodies just like we can leave a house.
The spirit leaves when the body stops working.
The spirit goes somewhere else.
We don't know for sure where the spirit goes.
Some people believe that the spirits of people who die go to heaven.
This is a nice place to think of.
It is okay to think of the people we love being in heaven after their bodies are dead.
Heaven would be a very happy and safe place to be.

Different **cultures**, **religions** and **belief systems** have different names for the happy and safe places where loved ones go after death. Some of these names include **Paradise**, **Tian**, **Moksha**, and **Valhalla**. Sometimes, people call the place that a person's spirit or **soul** goes after death simply the "**afterlife**." You may have heard someone say that your loved one "crossed over to the other side," has "gone home to God," or other similar things that seem to communicate that the person has gone to another place. This can seem confusing to some people, because the body has not gone anywhere. When people talk about a loved one going to **heaven**, "crossing over," or "going home," or any of the other expressions that people say when someone has died, what they mean is the person's spirit or soul, not the person's body.

Many people, of all different religions and cultures, believe that the **essence** of who a person is as an individual is not a physical body, but his or her spirit, or soul. The belief is that because the spirit or soul does not need the body to continue to exist, it leaves the body after the body has died. The belief is also that a body that has died can no longer hold a spirit or soul. This belief is explained above as the spirit leaving the body, as we might leave a house.

The belief that the spirit or the soul leaves the body after the body has died, is also the belief that the spirit or soul can live on peacefully and happily. Because of this, many people believe in happy and safe places that spirits go to live once they leave their bodies behind. There are also people and families who do *not* believe in places like heaven. Some people believe that once a person dies, that person's existence as a person is finished. These beliefs are okay too. In these cases, grieving people who do not believe in an afterlife may find comfort in other kinds of knowledge. They may find comfort in knowing that their loved one is not in pain. They may find comfort in the memories they have of the person they love who died. They may also find comfort in knowing that the body of their loved one will **decompose**, return to the earth, and become part of nature's ongoing cycle of birth, life, and death. All living things, including people, plants, and animals that die will decompose and become part of the earth in a different form.

People who do not believe in an afterlife may also be comforted by the proven principle of physics which tells us that energy can never die or be destroyed. It only changes form. It is a scientific fact that when a person is alive, that person's energy moves his or her body, pumps blood through veins and causes oxygen to move in and out of the lungs. Energy is the source of all the functions of the body and mind. Once a person dies, energy no longer exists in the body. A dead body neither requires nor uses energy. Because energy cannot be destroyed, we can know that the energy that was once inside the person we loved who has died, still exists. We may not understand or know how, or in what form, the energy exists, but we know through science that it does. This fact, whether a person believes in an afterlife or any kind of heaven, or not, can bring comfort to many people.

Beliefs about places like heaven are usually part of a person's or a family's belief system. Often what people believe about what happens to people after death is directly related to what they have learned from their parents and in their family traditions. Sometimes this might include a particular religion, sometimes not. No matter what the belief system, most families and cultures have practices and traditions that include particular rituals.

A ritual is an activity or a set of activities people engage in to help us feel calmer and more orderly, and which can also help us cope with difficult feelings. Some rituals are things a person does every day to help bring order and create a calm feeling. Some examples of daily rituals are things like brushing your teeth at the same time each morning, or laying your clothes out nightly before bed to help you have a calmer, more orderly morning. Rituals to help us remember the people we love who have died are different from our daily rituals that we do to help us create order in our day. They are similar in that they help us create some order in the chaos of feelings that grief can bring, but different because they can be more elaborate, and often include other people.

An example of a ritual that happens in many cultures after someone dies is the funeral. You may have attended a funeral for your loved one. Not everyone has a funeral. Sometimes other kinds of rituals happen after a person dies. Sometimes the person who died may have written down or communicated in some other way about what they wanted to happen after their death. When this happens, families try to do what the person said he or she wanted to happen after their death. If a person has not communicated what he or she wants to happen after their death, family members usually try very hard to do what they think the person who died would want. It is a good thing for people to communicate about what they want to happen to their bodies after their deaths. It is good for families to talk about these things. If people talk about these topics, it can sometimes make things easier for family members after someone has died. Sometimes, though, if a baby, a child, or very young person dies, or if a death happens very suddenly, people do not have a chance to talk about these things first. It is always good to do what is **respectful** and what shows love and care for the person who has died.

The following section gives information about some of the different kinds of rituals that may happen after a person has died. You and your family may have participated in some of these kinds of rituals. You and your family may have participated in other kinds of rituals. There are many different customs, traditions and rituals that people participate in after a loved one dies.

Wakes, Viewings, and Visitations

Wakes were traditionally held in the home of the person who died, with the body present in the home. The reason the ritual is called a "wake" is that traditionally, the family would stay awake all night before the **burial**, and watch over or guard the body. Some people think that this was to make sure that the person was actually dead and that they would not "wake" up. In times when technology was not as good as it is now, sometimes doctors or family had a difficult time knowing whether someone had actually died. There may have been times when a person was very ill and thought to be dead, but then recovered. Others say that this is not the case, but rather that the word "wake" came from a word that meant "to watch or guard." Either way, the family stayed at home with the body of the loved one. Extended family and friends would come to the home to visit, and to "pay their respects" to the dead. To "pay respects" is an expression in the English language that means to show admiration or honor toward a person. Usually people would bring food and offer support and comfort to those who were grieving.

Wakes rarely happen in family homes in modern times. Currently, wakes usually happen at a funeral home with the body present. The family announces what time they will receive visitors, and extended family and friends come. There is usually a guest book for people to sign so the family can remember who came to visit.

A **viewing** is the same thing as a wake, but the name implies that the **casket**, or the **coffin**, will be open so that visitors will be able to see the body of the person who died. People are allowed to touch, or even kiss, the body of the person if they choose. This is an okay and safe thing to do. Whether a person wants to touch, or even look at the body is a very personal decision. It is okay for people to look at or touch the body. It is also okay if a person chooses not to look at or touch the body. It is also okay to look, but choose not to touch.

Visitation is the same as a wake, or a viewing, except the coffin or casket is usually closed. Whether a family calls this ritual a wake, visitation, or viewing, often depends on where they live, and sometimes on their religion.

Often at wakes, viewings, and visitations, and other rituals, people hug the family members of the person who died. Other visitors, extended family, and friends, may also hug each other. Some people find comfort in hugging and in being hugged. Sometimes hugging may seem to cause a person to begin to cry. This is okay. It is also okay if people do not want to be hugged. Many people with ASD do not like to be hugged. If you are one of those people, it is okay to say, "I do not like to be hugged, but thank you." This is a **polite** way to let someone know that you would rather not be hugged. If you would rather shake hands or give a high five or a fist bump, you can offer that to the person as well. A good rule for most people to follow is to ask whether it is okay to hug. A person might say, "Is it okay if I hug you?" or "Can I give you a hug?" In this way, it makes it easier for a person to say yes or no to hugs. You may want to follow this rule if you like to hug other people. If you want to be hugged, it is also okay to ask a trusted person, a family member, caregiver, or good friend, for a hug.

Funeral

A funeral is a ritual that is usually held in a church, temple, mosque, or other religious building. Funerals can also be held outdoors. A funeral happens fairly soon after a person's death, usually within a week. At a funeral there is usually someone who speaks, or several people may speak. Often, a minister, pastor, priest, rabbi, or other religious leader will speak and offer prayers. Other people, family and friends may also speak. There may be one or many speakers. Usually the speakers talk about good memories of the person who died. They usually also talk about why the person who died was important and loved. There are also usually prayers, singing, or music at a funeral. Pictures of the person who died may be present as well. Usually at a funeral, the person's body is present, in a coffin or a casket. A coffin and a casket mean the same thing. It is a box, made of wood or metal, which holds the body after death. The inside of the coffin or casket is often padded and soft to protect the body. Even though the body can no longer feel pain or cold or any sensation at all, people who love the person want to take care of and protect the body. This is a good thing and shows that the person was loved.

The coffin or casket may be open or closed at the funeral. This is a personal choice for the family or for the person who died. He or she may have made it known that they would prefer an open or a closed casket. If the casket is open, there is usually a time for the people attending the funeral to stand next to the coffin or casket and "pay their respects." This means a short period for each person to see the person's body, and to remember the person in his or her own way. As at a wake or a viewing, some people choose to touch the body, or even kiss the body. This is a very personal choice. It is okay and safe to do this. Often, people may also choose to place items into the casket or coffin with the body. They may place letters, pictures, the person's favorite things into the casket. While people know that the dead body can no longer use these things, the gestures are symbolic and express love and care for the person who has died.

After the funeral, usually the body is buried, and the family and others present at the funeral may go to the burial or **interment** site. In some religious traditions, including Judaism and Islam, the body is buried within 24 hours. (Also, in Islamic tradition, coffins or caskets are not used. The body is wrapped in sheets of clean, white cloth.) In these religious traditions, the funeral rituals must also take place quickly.

Burial and interment places usually occur at a **cemetery** (also sometimes called a **graveyard**) or a **mausoleum**. Mausoleums are usually located inside cemeteries, but they may also be found in churches, temples, or other religious buildings. A mausoleum is a building or structure, usually made of stone or brick, that holds secure, safe above-ground places for bodies of the dead to be placed. Sometimes these may be small spaces with individual stone crypts (very strong, secure chambers that each hold the body of a person who died), or there may be walls of strong, safe compartments that will hold the body of a person who died. There may be many bodies interred at public mausoleums, or the mausoleum may be small and private, used only by one family.

Graveside Service or Committal Service

A **graveside service**, or **committal service**, can happen after a funeral, or instead of funeral. Some families have a funeral at a religious building (church, temple, or mosque) and a graveside or committal service following the funeral. The service is sometimes called a committal service because the body, if it is buried in the ground, is "committed to the earth." To commit, in this sense, means to "give to, to place, or entrust to" the earth. What a family chooses to call the service depends again on where the family is from, and what the traditions of the family have been in the past.

At a graveside or committal service, the casket or coffin is brought to the cemetery or mausoleum and the family and friends gather around. Often chairs will have been placed near the grave site or near the tomb or burial chamber. Sometimes lowering the casket or coffin into the ground is part of the service, sometimes not. If the casket is lowered into the ground as part of the service, the minister or other religious leader may toss a handful of earth onto the casket to symbolize the earth covering the body. Family members may also toss symbolic handfuls of dirt onto the casket. In some religious and cultural traditions, family members may fill the entire grave themselves. If the lowering of the casket into the grave is not a part of the service, family and friends may also place flowers onto the casket to be lowered into the grave. There may also be prayers, speaking or singing.

At some interment services there is no casket or coffin. If the body of the person has been cremated, there is no need for a large casket. **Cremation** is the practice of reducing a dead body to ashes by burning. In communicating their wishes for what will happen after their deaths, many people choose for their bodies to be cremated. Some families choose this option for their loved one if their loved one's wishes were not known. It is important to remember that a dead body feels no pain. It is never painful for a person to be cremated after death. When people are cremated, the body is usually placed into a crematory box. The box is usually made of wood or sturdy cardboard. Some people choose to have items placed into the box with the person, such as pictures or letters. The box and the body are placed in a closed chamber where both the box and the body are burned at very high temperatures. When the chamber cools, the body and the box, and any other contents, are reduced to ash. This ash is called the crematory remains, or simply "remains."

The family is given the remains in a special box, or in a crematory urn, a special container just for the purpose of holding the remains of a cremated body. Some families keep the urn in a special place in their homes. Some choose to have the remains, along with the urn or box, interred in a burial spot or mausoleum. Some family members may choose to "scatter the ashes." This means to distribute the remains in a particular place. This usually involves pouring or gently tossing the remains out of the special container. A family may scatter the ashes in a place that the person specified before he or she died. If the person did not make their wishes known, the family may also choose a place they believe the person would be happy about. It is usually a place that was special to the person or a place where he or she liked to spend time. Some people scatter ashes on the ocean or another body of water, they may spread them in a garden, stand on a mountain top and let the wind carry the ashes across the treetops. Some family members may choose to keep a small bit of the remains and wear them in a piece of special jewelry made just for that purpose, or they may choose to keep some of the remains in a smaller special container. Any of these things is okay and good to do.

Often, after the funeral, burial or interment service, extended family and friends will gather at the home of the person who died to share food and spend time together. Sometimes these gatherings may happen at another place. Some places families may choose to gather after a service might be the church or temple recreational space, a fellowship hall, a restaurant, or someone else's home. People usually share food, and they may also cry, hug, laugh, and share memories or photographs of the person who died or other family members. They may also talk about other family members who have died. Often, people may travel from far away and will not have seen each other for a while. These gatherings are meant to help the family know people are there to support and comfort the grieving family members and each other.

Memorial Service

A **memorial service** can be held at any time after a person's death. The body of the person who died is usually not present for a memorial service. Memorial services can be held anywhere. Sometimes they are held in a church, temple, or other religious building, but they are often held outdoors, at people's homes, at parks, even theaters or restaurants. Sometimes memorial services are held at places where the person who died loved to go when they were alive. As at a funeral, people usually speak at a memorial service. Many people may speak and share stories about the one who died. Memorial services may also include prayer and singing or music. Often, people will read passages from books or they may share letters they have written to the person. A memorial service is usually less formal than a funeral. Videos or photo slide shows may be shown, but at least one picture of the person who died is usually present. Sometimes there is food served at the memorial service and people who attend the service will stay after the service to spend time with each other, share memories, and provide comfort and support to each other and the grieving family members. Sometimes, family and friends may go to a restaurant or other place to spend time together after the memorial service.

Celebration of Life

A **celebration of life** is similar to a funeral or a memorial service. People who have a celebration of life want to focus on all the wonderful things about the person who died, and celebrate the fact that the person was alive. They want to celebrate the fact that they knew the person and that they shared in the person's life in some way. There is often music played and happy, funny stories are shared. The atmosphere is festive. A celebration of life may also include videos and pictures of the person and his or her friends and family. A celebratory atmosphere does not mean that the people who participate are not sad. They will miss the person who died and there may also be sadness. It is okay to be happy and sad at the same time. As in the memorial service, often there is food and drink either at the celebration itself, or family and friends gather at another place to share food and drink and spend time together.

Some of the rituals above have to do with what happens to the person's body after death, some of them are about ways that family and friends honor the memory of their loved one. All of them are meant to help the family and loved ones who are grieving feel supported and loved. There are many other rituals and traditions besides the ones listed above. You and your family may have participated in some of the above rituals. Your family, culture or religion may have different rituals.

Rituals like those you may have seen or participated in after your loved one died, are more symbolic and are the type of rituals that people engage in to mark important occasions, honor a loved one's memory. Rituals exist and are created to allow people a special time to remember loved ones, to help people through feeling difficult emotions, and enable them to have support from other people. Rituals can also help people to get used to the fact that someone has died.

Sometimes rituals can be large, traditional events, like a funeral or memorial service, or they might be very small and made up especially by someone who wants to remember a loved one. You, or any other person who chooses to do so, can create a ritual for remembering and honoring a loved who has died. Some examples of these kinds of creative and personal rituals are listed in Chapter 9.

Traditions and Rituals in My Family

You may want to write down the different kinds of traditions and rituals your family participated in after your loved one died. You can use the space below if you like, or you can write in your journal or notebook.

These are the rituals or traditions that my family participated in after _____ *died:*

. . . .

. . . .

. . . .

. . . .

I have some questions about some of the rituals and traditions that my family participated in after _____ *died. They are:*

. . . .

. . . .

. . . .

. . . .

Draw or paint a picture of what you think heaven, or the afterlife, might be like. Imagine a happy and safe place that you believe would be a good place for your loved one. Depending on what you and your family believe in, you might choose to call this place heaven, or you might want to give your loved one's happy and safe place a different name.

What kinds of things would be in the happy and safe place for your loved one? Are there animals there? Plants? Are there other people? Is it completely different from anything we might see here on Earth? If you or your family believes in a specific kind of heaven, you can imagine that place. If your family does not believe in a place like heaven, think about what sort of place you would like to imagine your loved one being in now.

Use any size paper you like and whatever **medium** you like best. In art, a medium is what you choose to make your art with.

If you like, you can write a story or a poem about heaven or the place where you would like to imagine your loved one is now. This is your creation and your wish for your loved one's happy and safe place. You can make it however you like. Hang your picture somewhere you can see it. When you look at it, you can be reminded of your loved one feeling safe and happy.

Figure 4.1 Here is an example of a young lady's drawing of heaven. She created it while thinking of a place where she would like to imagine her grandfather now living peacefully. He died when she was much younger. (Drawing by Ashley Morris.)

Chapter 5

It's Okay to Feel Sad, or Even Angry, When Someone We Love Dies

It's okay to feel sad, or even angry, when someone we love dies.

It's okay to feel many different feelings at the same time. Sadness and anger are very common, but they are not the only feelings you might have when someone you love dies. Some other feelings might include afraid, frustrated, lonely, worried, anxious, curious, and many more. Sometimes it can be confusing to try to know just exactly what you are feeling. This is okay too. You can say you feel confused.

Naming My Feelings

Make a list of the different feelings you have had since your loved one has died. You can use this page, or you can make your own sheet, or write it down in your journal. You can write down the feelings you feel all at the same time on the same line or on separate lines. You can date the different feelings that you have, or have had, or you can write a short sentence about when you felt that way. You may also want to use your Body Map to help you remember some of your feelings. You don't have to fill up all the lines, or you may need more space—either of those things is okay.

Since _____ died, I have felt:

. . . .

. . . .

. . . .

. . . .

. . . .

. . . .

. . . .

Drawing My Feelings

After you make your list, choose a feeling and draw a picture of what that particular feeling looks like for you. You can choose just one feeling, or as many as you like. You can make a series of drawings or paintings of all your different feelings if you choose. Use crayons, markers, pencils, pens, paints, oil pastels, or a mix of different mediums (remember, a medium is what you choose to make your art with). You can draw as many pictures of as many of your feelings as you want. You can hang them on the wall, on the refrigerator, keep them in your journal, or you can share them with people you love and trust.

Feelings of Sadness

Everyone feels sad sometimes. It is okay to feel sad. Sadness is an emotion people feel when we lose something, when we are disappointed, or when a hurtful thing has happened to us, or to someone else we care about. Any combination of those things can cause us to feel sadness. Sometimes we may not understand all the reasons we are feeling sad. When people we love die, we might feel sad a lot of the time. You might feel sad every day, or part of every day, for a while. Every person experiences grief differently because we are all individual people, each with our own individual feelings. Each person who is grieving grieves in his or her own way. But we all feel sad when someone we love, and who is important to us, dies. You may feel as though you are all alone. You may feel that there is nothing to look forward to. You may feel that the world is no longer a happy or safe place. It can be helpful to know that this feeling will not last forever and it will pass. It is okay to feel this way when someone you love has died.

Things You Can Do That Might Help Yourself Feel Better When You Feel Sad

- **Cry.** Crying sometimes can feel scary because you may feel so sad that you think your tears might never stop. But this is not true. No matter how much or how long you cry, eventually the tears will stop. Many times, crying can help us feel better after we cry. Some people like to cry with a friend or trusted person who can help them feel safe and comforted, other people like to cry alone. It is also okay if you do not cry. *Not* crying does not mean that you do not care that your loved one has died. *Not* crying does not mean that you do not miss him or her.

- **Talk to someone you trust about your feelings.** Sometimes when we talk about our sad feelings we might find that they seem to slowly melt away. If you cannot talk about your feelings, move on to the next suggestion.

- **Write your feelings down.** You can write them in a letter or in your journal. You can make a list of words that are close to describing your feelings. You can share your writing about your feelings with someone you trust if you wish.

- **Draw a picture of your sadness.** What would it look like? What colors would it be? If it came alive, would it look like an animal? What shapes would it take? Would it look like something in nature? Might it look like something completely and totally original to you?

- **Go outside and find at least five things that you think are beautiful.** Draw a picture of those things or write a poem, essay, journal entry, or a story about those things.

- **Listen to your favorite music.**

- **Move your body around.** Dance, stretch, jump around, take big steps, wave your arms around fast or slow, bend forward, march, skip, or walk in strange ways. Let your body move around in whatever ways feel good. You can use music, or make up your own music, or move in silence. All of these are good to do.

- **Sing your favorite song.**

- **Play dress up.** Dress up in a funny costume, wear a fake mustache, paint your face with face paint, do your hair in a wild and crazy style, pile on lots of jewelry or awesome sunglasses, wear a really cool hat, or put on your dressiest outfit and best shoes. You may want to go around like this for the rest of the day and see how people react! You can write about it in your journal if you want to.

- **Ask someone you enjoy spending time with to go with you** to the park, a museum, the zoo, or to any fun place that you like to visit.

- **Ask someone to go to a funny movie with you.** You can also watch funny movies on television, computer or DVD. Make sure you have popcorn and your favorite drinks! Remember that it is okay to laugh, even after someone we love has died.

Laughter makes us feel good. Scientific research has proven that laughter is good for our bodies and our minds.

- **Hug people you love or ask for a hug from someone you love.** Remember that it is okay to feel like you are going to start crying while you are hugging. Sometimes when we get hugs when we are sad, the hug can make us feel like crying. This is okay, it means the hugs are working to help you feel better. It is also okay to *not* cry when you are hugging. It is also okay to not hug, if you do not like hugs. If other people want to hug you and you do not want a hug, it is okay to tell them that you would rather not hug. You can do this in a polite and respectful way.

- **Ask someone to help you bake cookies.**

- **Eat some cookies with very cold milk or your favorite drink.**

- **Pack up some of the cookies, decorate the package, and then give them to a neighbor or a friend**, or someone else you know who might be feeling sad too.

- **Hula hoop!**

- **Think of something nice to do for someone else and then do it.** Write about it or draw a picture to remember this nice thing you did for someone else.

- **Make a card for someone.**

- **Spend a day taking pictures of people and things that you like.** You can do this alone or with someone else. You can save the pictures and later make a **collage**. You can look at your collage when you are feeling sad on another day or whenever you like. See Chapter 8 for suggestions about making a collage.

- **Make a list of things that you feel grateful for.** Gratitude is a feeling people experience when we are thankful (or **grateful**) for people, things and events in our lives which make us feel happy, safe, peaceful, and good. These things can be anything you can think of that you are grateful for and happy to have in your life. Those things might include flowers, sunshine, crayons, cartoons, your friends, birthday cake, people who love you, your pet, music, games, baseball, trains, your family, school, vacation, weather reports, books, a warm place to sleep, good food, your eyeglasses, snow, computers, holidays. The list could be very long! You can start your own list and add to it whenever you want. You may want to set aside some pages in your journal just for a special Gratitude List, or have a whole different book just for your Gratitude Journal. At the ending of each day, you may want to think about at least five things for which you were grateful. You can also make a Gratitude Journal especially for good things that happen to you each day. No matter how hard a day is, we can usually think of something that happened that made us feel good in the day at some time.

Also, please remember that you don't have to do anything that makes you uncomfortable. Choose activities that you think will help you feel better. If you are doing an activity that makes you feel bad, you can stop. This might happen if the activity brings up sad or upsetting feelings. You can stop and start again later, or just choose not to do that activity.

Can you think of some other things that you like to do to make yourself feel better when you are sad? Write them in your journal or list them here:

. . . .

. . . .

. . . .

. . . .

. . . .

Feeling Angry

Everyone feels angry sometimes. It is okay to feel angry. Anger is a signal to us that something is wrong in our **environment**. Your environment is made up of all the people, things, and places that surround you. When we are hurt or frustrated, we may become angry. When we do not know what to do in a situation, we may become angry. When we feel powerless to change things, we may become angry. Sometimes anger can feel unpleasant or even scary, but sometimes it can be very helpful. Anger is helpful when it serves as a **catalyst** to help us change things in our lives that need to be changed. A catalyst is something that causes a change. Sometimes, though, we are unable to change the things that make us angry. When someone you love dies and you feel angry, you cannot change the fact that the person you love has died. When you are angry and cannot change the situation, then you must try to change your anger instead of the situation. Sometimes, it is hard to simply change the way we feel by thinking about it. Most people must *do* something different to change the way they are feeling. A way to change your anger is to get your anger out in a safe way. It is not good for people to be angry for long periods of time. When you feel angry, and cannot change the situation, there are things you can do to help yourself feel better. Remember, it is okay to feel angry. What matters most is what you decide to do when you are angry. The most important thing is to stay safe. Sometimes when we are angry, we may want to do things that are unsafe or bad for us or other people. Anything that is unsafe or harmful to yourself or others is a wrong and dangerous thing to do.

How can you know when you are angry?

- **Use what you learned from doing your Body Map** to help you know when you are feeling angry. The information you learned in that exercise can help you understand places in your body where you hold strong feelings. Those places may be where you feel anger in your body first. Being more aware of your body and how it feels is a good thing.

- **Look at your hands.** Are they relaxed or clenched? Clenched hands often indicate anger.

- **Notice your breathing.** Is it normal or relaxed? Is it fast and uneven? Fast, uneven breathing often indicates anger.

- **Pay attention to your belly.** Does it feel like it usually feels or does it feel like it is tightening up? Does it feel hot inside? Or like you are holding something heavy in your belly? Or does it feel knotted up? Does it feel like it has butterflies inside? Any of those changes can indicate anger.

- **Pay attention to your chest.** Does it feel like it usually feels or does it feel tight? Does it feel like your heart is being squeezed or like you can't breathe deeply? These are also changes that can indicate anger.

- **Check your face.** Does it look normal or is it turning red and feeling hot? Does it have an angry expression? Are your eyebrows drawn inward toward your nose, or is your forehead scrunched up? Is your mouth relaxed or tight? Learning how your face looks when you have different feelings can be helpful. You can ask a trusted person to take pictures of you when you have different expressions on your face and you can label them according to the feeling. This can help you be more aware of your own feelings and how you show them to others.

Safe Ways to Get Your Anger Out

- **Take deep breaths.** Breathing deep into your belly, or your **diaphragm**, can help anger soften more quickly. Your diaphragm is located just behind your belly button. It is made up of strong muscles that protect your belly area and let your lungs fill with air. First, pull your muscles in toward your middle as you **exhale** (or breathe out), to help squeeze out all the stale air from your lungs. Then, as you **inhale** (or breathe in), let your belly area fill up with air first, and then fill your chest. Hold it for five counts and let it out with a big sigh. Do this several times. This might be easier to do while lying down. A very good way to learn to breathe deep into your belly is to think of your very favorite thing to smell. Imagine that you are taking a great big, deep smell of this favorite scent. When we smell something we love to smell, we automatically breathe deep into our bellies.

You should practice your deep breathing every day, when you are calm. This way, it is easier for your body to remember how to do it when you are angry or upset. The best time to practice deep breathing is when you are relaxed, while you are lying on the floor looking a book, or just before a nap or bedtime. It can also help you to fall asleep at night.

- **Squeeze and release your muscles.** Tighten up all your muscles all over your body and take a deep breath in and hold it. Keep your muscles tight and hold your breath as long as you can and then...whoosh!...let it all out and let all your muscles go totally loose. Do this a few times until you feel that your anger has passed. This is another good thing to practice when you are relaxed so that you can remember how to do it when you are upset or angry. When you learn where your muscle groups are located—feet and legs, hands and arms, torso, shoulders, and the muscles of the face—and how they feel different when they are tense and when relaxed, it is much easier to tell when anger is causing your muscles to tense up. It is also easier to relax your muscles when you have already practiced. Tensing and relaxing your muscle groups is also a good thing to do at bedtime to help you sleep better.

- **Count.** Count as high as you want, starting from 0 or 1. You can also start with a really high number and count backward. If you know another language, count forward and backward in that language. Count in whatever way you like.

- **Twist a towel, or pull on a towel with a friend.**

- **Paint or draw big, colorful, angry pictures.** Make angry sounds while you draw or paint. When you're finished with your angry pictures, put them in the freezer for a while to let them cool off! Putting your anger in the freezer is a symbolic way of cooling down the real anger that you feel in your body. Once the angry pictures are in the freezer, you can lie down and imagine your anger being cooled and frozen. We know from scientific studies that people who imagine these kinds of things can actually cause real changes inside their bodies. Another thing you can do is place your angry picture into a sealable freezer bag with something heavy, like stones. Try to get as much air out of the bag as possible. Place your picture in a container of water and let it sink to the bottom. Freeze the whole container of water. Once it is frozen, take it out and see how long it takes the ice to melt away. Again you can imagine that the ice is melting away your angry feelings.

- **Ask permission to dig a hole.** Once you have finished, begin to concentrate on your anger. Bring it all up to your hands and fingertips. Imagine throwing it in the hole, or letting it drain slowly out of your fingers into the hole. You can hold a piece of paper, a piece of fruit, or something else that is biodegradable in your hands and imagine putting your anger into that object. Put your anger and the object, if you are using one, into the hole. Fill the hole in and bury your anger. Be sure to thank the Earth for taking your anger from you.

- **Write your anger down in your journal to keep and read later.** Write your anger down on different paper that you can tear up and destroy.

- **Run as fast as you can.** Do this in a place indoors, or outside at a park, or a track, in a gymnasium, etc. Stop when you feel ready, or too tired to go on, and then lie down on the ground or the floor. Imagine your anger slowly ooze out of your body as you rest. Each time you exhale, imagine more of your anger melting out of your body, like butter or hot candle wax. Imagine it being absorbed into the floor, through the floor, and then into the ground below you. Remember to thank the Earth for taking your anger from you.

- **Jump up and down, and stomp your feet.** Continue to jump and stomp until you are tired, and then fall to the ground, or onto the floor. Let your anger melt out of your body, into the Earth below.

- **Squeeze a pillow or a rolled up blanket with your arms or legs as hard as you can.**

- **Pretend that you are an animal and then act out what you imagine that animal would do if it were angry**—howl, screech, growl, hiss, roar, run, jump, pounce, roll around, and shake your body.

- **Squeeze and mash chunks of clay.** Throw your chunks at a brick wall, onto a hard floor (not carpets or rugs), or onto a table. As you squeeze your clay chunks, you can imagine pressing and pushing your angry feelings into the balls of clay. Imagine your anger becoming squashed as the clay is smashed against the hard surface. Make sure you have permission to do this, clay can be messy. You may also decide to make a clay sculpture of what your anger looks like. This could be anything. It might take an abstract form, an animal form, a human form, or any form that seems to mirror what you feel your anger would like at that moment. You can choose to save your sculpture, or you may choose to break it up into bits. It is your decision. If you let your clay sculpture dry and then smash it, wear protective eye wear (like goggles) so no dry clay fragments get into your eyes.

- **Ask an adult to take you someplace safe where you can throw rocks as hard and as far as you can.** Throwing rocks into water can be particularly satisfying. Hold each rock between both of your hands before you throw it and imagine sending your anger into the rock. When you let the rock fly, yell out loud! You can choose a word to yell, or you can just make a loud yelling sound. Throwing rocks into a body of water may seem so satisfying because we are making a big splash! When we feel very small and powerless, proof that we can still make a big splash—even with rocks in the water—can make us feel a bit better.

- **Ask an adult to help you find some small water balloons.** Water balloons are sold at most big variety stores, or party stores, and sometimes at drug stores or grocery stores. Fill your balloons with water and tie them off. Get a big bowl or bucket to hold your balloons. Use a permanent marker in your color of choice to write words or draw pictures on the filled balloons to represent your angry feelings. Remember that you must stay calm while handling and writing on your balloons! You don't want them to burst until you are ready to really let fly! You can use your breathing to help you stay calm. When you are finished writing and drawing on your balloons, take them outside. Ask permission to throw them someplace where it is safe to do this. You might choose to throw them at a big tree, the driveway, a plank fence, or a side of the house that has no windows.

  Choose a balloon. Hold the balloon in your hands and concentrate on the word or picture you have drawn onto the balloon. Pull up all the angry feelings you have that are associated with the word or image on that balloon. Imagine the anger leaving your body to fill up the balloon in place of the water. When the balloon is full of your anger, throw it as hard as you can and watch it burst. (Be careful not to squeeze the balloon too hard before you throw or it can burst in your hands.) As you throw, you might want to yell out an angry sound, or the word you wrote on the balloon. Make sure to clean up all the burst balloon pieces.

Make a Scream Box

To make your scream box you will need:

- a cardboard box—a shoe box or a cereal box can work

- paint, crayons, markers, wrapping paper, pictures cut from magazines, yarn, stickers, anything you would like to use for decorating your box

- some old rags, cotton balls, or newspaper (rags and cotton material seem to work best)

- a paper towel tube

- duct tape or packing tape.

Figure 5.1 Things you will need for your scream box.

To make your scream box:

1. Stuff the box at least halfway full with the rags, cotton, newspaper, or whatever you decide to use that will absorb the sound of the scream.

2. Decide where you want the opening to be. Place the paper towel tube in the space and trace around the tube with a marker so that you will know where to cut.

3. Cut the hole so the paper towel tube can go part way into the box. Be very careful cutting the hole. Ask an adult to help you if necessary.

4. Insert the paper towel tube into the hole. Tape around the base of the opening and at least part of the tube to seal it shut. You can tape all the way up the tube if you like, to make it stronger. Tape around the box top or lid of the box to seal it shut.

5. Decorate the box, including the tube, however you like. You can paint it, wrap it in plain or colored paper, write words on it, draw pictures, use stickers, glitter, glue, strands of yarn. Use whatever you like.

Figure 5.2 Photo of taped tube on wrapped box[1].

Figure 5.3 Decorating the box.

1   A tip: If you want to wrap your entire box in paper, it may be helpful to do this first, before cutting the hole and inserting your tube.

Figure 5.4 Finished scream box!

To use your Scream Box:

Hold onto the tube, put it to your mouth and scream!!

You might want to make scream boxes for other people who might also be missing someone they love too. They might feel like screaming sometimes too!

Remember, you can do any of these activities until you feel your anger has left you or until you start laughing! Some of them can be pretty funny, especially if you do them with a friend or a trusted adult. Laughter is a great cure for angry feelings. Remember that it's okay to laugh, even after someone we love has died.

Things That Make Me Feel Better

Can you think of some other things that you like to do to make yourself feel better when you are angry? Write them in your journal or list them here:

. . . .

. . . .

. . . .

. . . .

. . . .

. . . .

. . . .

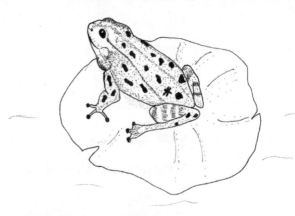

Chapter 6

It's Okay to Miss the People We Love

When someone we love dies, we miss them.
It is okay to miss the people we love.

Missing the people we love when they are away from us is hard. When someone we love has died, missing them can be very painful because we know that we will not see them again. When people miss someone they love, they usually try to connect with those people in some way, by phone, email, or the postal service, through cards and letters. When we miss the people we love, we like to tell them that we miss them and that we love them. We like to share what we've been doing, and tell them about the things that are happening in our lives. You can still talk to the one you love who has died and tell them all these things and more. You can tell them anything you like. Here are some ways you can **communicate** your feelings to your loved one:

Write a Letter

You can write a letter to your loved one anytime you want. You can write down whatever you are feeling. Tell them how much you love and miss them. Tell them how you are doing. About what is going on in your life, in your family, at school, whatever you like.

If you can't think of what to write, you could use this letter worksheet:

Dear _____,

I always wanted to tell you

. . . .

. . . .

. . . .

I would have liked to

. . . .

. . . .

. . . .

I would like

. . . .

. . . .

. . . .

I hope that

. . . .

. . . .

. . . .

Thank you for

. . . .

. . . .

. . . .

✓   Love,

_____

What to do with your letters

Once you have written your letter, you may not know what to do with it.

- You can bury your letter in a forest next to a beautiful tree. Be sure to thank the tree and the land for taking your letter for you.

- You can ask permission to bury your letter in a small hole that you dig at the gravesite of your loved one.

- You can ask an adult to help you burn the letter in a safe way. Many cultures believe that the rising smoke from the letters as they burn can help carry our words to our loved ones.

- You might decide to keep the letter to read on special days, like your loved one's birthday or the anniversary of the death. Or you may decide not to read it at all, but to keep it in a special place.

Take a Walk With Your Loved One

Go outside in your yard, or to a park, or another nice walking area. You can ask an adult you trust to come with you. If you are in a safe area and have permission, you can walk by yourself. You can even take a walk around your own back yard. Bring a picture of your loved one along with you, if you want to. As you walk, remember your loved one who has died. Hold or look at the picture you brought. Use your imagination and pretend that you are walking beside the one you miss. Begin to talk to your loved one. You can say whatever you like.

"Talk" on the Phone With Your Loved One

Just because your loved one may not talk back in a way your ears can hear, doesn't mean that you cannot say all the things that you would like to say to him or her. And you can imagine what might be said back to you. You can speak for them or imagine that you hear his or her voice in your mind. Sometimes holding a phone to our ear and talking to our loved ones helps us to imagine conversations we might have. To do this you can use a real cell phone that is not turned on, a landline phone that is unplugged, or a toy phone. You can make your own pretend cell phone that you can carry around with you wherever you like. Making your own phone is nice because you can keep it just for the purpose of talking to your loved one whenever you wish. Making it can be something you do in honor of your loved one.

Make a Pretend Cell Phone

To make your own phone you will need:

- two empty snack-sized raisin boxes—or use only one raisin box if you would like your phone to be smaller and not the "flip" type

- a picture of a cell phone—you can draw one, or you can find a picture in a magazine to cut out, photograph a real cell phone, or find an image online, print and cut it to fit the length of your boxes placed end to end

- paint—whatever color you want your phone to be

- glue or acrylic gel medium—I prefer acrylic gel medium because it lasts longer and goes on more smoothly

- clear packing tape.

Figure 6.1 Supplies to make your pretend cell phone.

To make your pretend cell phone:

1. First, paint your raisin boxes whatever color you like and let them dry.

2. When they are dry, put the bottom edge of one box to the bottom edge of the second box so that it creates a triangle shape—this will be your hinge.

3. Place a piece of tape on the front of the first box with enough excess to hang down from the bottom. Hold your tape away from the second box until you line up your edges, then press the tape smoothly down over the front of the second box. The tape should be holding the boxes together from one side, but open on the other, so that you can "flip" the phone open and closed.

4. Glue your picture of the cell phone that you have drawn, printed or cut out onto the taped front of the box.

Figure 6.2 Painting the boxes.

Figure 6.3 Creating the hinge.

Figure 6.4 Drawing of the cell phone glued and taped onto the hinged boxes.

If you like, after your picture is attached, you can use the clear tape to cover the entire phone, to protect it from dirt or damage for a bit longer.

Use your phone to talk to your loved one anytime you like. You can use your phone just for talking to the one you love and miss, or you can use it for other kinds of things—pretend talking with a friend, calling for pizza, or whatever you want!

Figure 6.5 Finished pretend cell phone.

Chapter 7

We Can Talk to Others about How We Feel

When we feel sad or angry we can talk about how we feel with friends, family, or others we trust, like a teacher or counselor.

Sometimes when we feel sad or angry, or when we miss someone who has died, we need to talk to a living person.

My Support People

Make a list of the people you have in your life who you can talk to when you feel that you need a living person to listen. You can write your list in your notebook or journal, or you can write the list here:

People I can Go to when I Need to Talk:

. . . .

. . . .

. . . .

. . . .

You don't have to fill up all the lines. If you like, you can write each person's phone number or how to reach them when you need them on your list as well.

Sometime soon after making your list of people you can go to when you need to talk, go to each of the people on your list and let them know that they are on your list of trusted listeners. Ask them if it is okay for you to have them on your list and if they will be willing to be there for you when you need to talk. When they say yes, remember to thank them. If they say no, or that they would rather not, or that they feel they cannot be a good listener, you can say something like, "Okay. I will ask someone else." Not everyone may feel that he or she can be a good listener. Usually, though, if you believe that a certain person will be good to have on your list, they will agree to be a good listener.

You may not feel there is anyone to talk to, or that the people you have talked to are not helpful. In this case, finding a **counselor** or therapist to talk to may be very beneficial. At the end of this book there is a resource section telling ways to find a good counselor to help with the pain of grief.

While it is true that talking about our feelings can be very helpful in releasing difficult feelings, talking is not the only way to communicate. Communication is the act of exchanging and sharing information. Often people do this by talking, but as you may have already learned in your life, and through the activities you've read about in this book, there are other ways to share and exchange information. Communication is also done through writing, art, dance, and other art forms. One person or a group of people sends the message they wish others to receive through a chosen method of communication. Here is a list of types of communication:

1. **Talking.** This is also known as verbal communication. This could be in person, on the phone, or over the computer using web-cameras.

2. **Writing.** This might include letters, short notes, essays, articles, journal or blog entries, books, or poetry.

3. **Sign language.** Sign language is a special kind of language using hand and finger movements as well as other body movements to communicate. The different kinds of sign language include American (ASL), French, British, Australian, New Zealand, and International Sign Languages. There are also other versions of these that may be specific to certain areas of the world.

4. **Body movement.** This can mean "body language," which includes facial expressions, posture of the body, gestures, and eye movements. Body language can be planned or unplanned. It can go along with other types of communication, such as talking or signing. Body movement can also include dance or other kinds of creative movement that convey a message.

5. **Other art forms**, such as painting, drawing, photography, computer or digital art, theater, singing, music, and performances of all kinds communicate information.

Thinking About Communication

Are there other types of communication that you can think of? You can write them below.

. . . .

. . . .

. . . .

What are your preferred ways to communicate? You can write them below.

I like to communicate in the following ways:

. . . .

. . . .

. . . .

Are there other ways that you might like to try to communicate? You can write them below.

I would like to try to communicate differently by using these ways:

. . . .

. . . .

. . . .

. . . .

It is important to remember that for communication to be successful, the person receiving the communication must understand what is being communicated. People with ASD sometimes have difficulty communicating. If you are one of those people, you may feel that others do not understand what you are trying to communicate. Sometimes you may feel that you do not understand what others are communicating to you. Sometimes you may think you know what is being communicated, and then discover you were wrong about what you thought was being communicated. This can be very frustrating.

Sometimes people with ASD can have particular problems with the body movement, or body language, type of communication (number 4 in the types of communications list). This might mean that you have difficulty understanding what someone else is communicating with body language or facial expression. Some people with ASD spend a lot of time trying to figure out what people are communicating with facial expressions and body language. Often the opposite kind of misunderstanding occurs; others may not understand *your* facial expression or body language. Many people with ASD can have body movements or facial expressions that seem to convey to others a message they have not intended. This usually happens more often if the person with ASD is under stress. For example, if you are feeling anxious or upset, you may laugh or smile instead of having a reaction that might seem more usual to many people. This also happens to other people who don't have ASD.

Stress, and especially grief, because grief is very stressful, can cause people to have reactions they typically would not have. These can show up on your face or in your body movements in ways that others may not understand. Sometimes others may assume (based on what they see on your face or in your body movements) that you are feeling or communicating something entirely different from what you are actually feeling or thinking. This might mean seeming "flat," or having a kind of blank facial expression, when others might typically expect crying, or very expressive facial movements. A non-ASD ("neurotypical," or "NT") reaction might be to interpret that you are not sad, that you are not feeling upset, or that you don't care, when in fact, you may be feeling something very deeply. Or, you may smile or laugh when you are actually feeling anxious or upset inside. That kind of reaction sometimes is a way to release stress or other painful feelings. Many people can misunderstand this kind of "opposite" stress reaction. Sometimes, if this kind of opposite reaction occurs, others may think it means that you are being rude, unfeeling, or uncaring. This is unfortunate, and so often, a very wrong assumption.

If you are aware that this happens to you, I recommend that you share this part of the book with someone you trust, someone who is a good communicator with you. If you are not aware that this happens to you, ask someone you trust if you have ever shown these kinds of "opposite" reactions to stressful situations and share this part of the book with them. If you are aware, or if you become aware, that your face and your body react in ways that are not typically what others expect, you can talk to people about it if you choose to do so. You might say something like, "I know I am not supposed to be laughing right now, but sometimes this is how my body deals with stress." Or, you could say something like, "I know it isn't how everyone deals with stressful feelings, but sometimes my face doesn't always look the way I feel on the inside." If you choose to do so, you can add, "I hope you don't think I am being rude." You might be surprised at other people's reactions to this kind of communication. Opening communication can increase understanding for everyone involved in a stressful situation. And you can't always rely on the grown-ups or the neurotypicals to do it. Sometimes they may have as much (or more!), trouble with communication as you do.

You can also continue reading and follow the guidelines in the next few paragraphs. Hopefully, they can help you to understand others better and help them to understand you. Understanding is the key to good communication.

Good, effective communication is important because, unless we communicate effectively, other people cannot know what we think or feel. It is important to share what we think and feel so that we can feel understood. When people feel understood, this can lead to a more peaceful life. When people make an effort to understand those around them, this can also lead to a more peaceful life.

To ensure good communication, it can be helpful to ask the person you are communicating with if they understand what you are communicating. It can be helpful for others to check with you as well, to be sure that you understand what they are communicating to you. If someone does not understand, the communicator can try to give more information or say things in a different way. If you do not understand something someone is communicating to you, it is okay to say, "Can you please tell me that again?" This way, the person will know that you did not understand. When others ask *you* to tell or explain things again, it is good to be patient and try to tell them again so that you feel understood and the person you are communicating with also understands what you are trying to communicate. Here are some other things you can say when you don't understand what is being communicated:

- "Can you say that in a different way?"

- "I don't understand what you are asking/telling me."

- "Can you ask me another way?"

- "Could you give me some more information about that?"

- "I'm not sure why you are asking that. Can you ask me a different question?"

Sometimes you may feel frustrated when you are communicating or when others are communicating with you. It is okay to feel frustrated. When this happens, it is good to try to let the person you are communicating with know how you are feeling. If you are feeling frustrated or stressed during a conversation, it is okay to say something like:

- "I am feeling overwhelmed."

- "I am feeling stressed right now."

- "Can we take a break for a minute?"

- "I need some time to think about this for a while."

- "Could I have some time to process what you are asking?"

It is important to understand each other, and to feel understood. When people understand each other, they can find out things they may never have known before. They may realize that even though people may be different from each other, there may be many things that they share or have in common. They may share likes or dislikes. They may enjoy similar things. They may find that they have thoughts, ideas, wishes, feelings, or fears in common. Finding out ways that people are similar can lead to deeper understanding of other people's experiences. This is true of people with or without ASD. This is true of people of all races, religions, ethnicities, and beliefs, with and without disabilities, from all over the world. It is true of all people.

When we are grieving, feeling understood can be important because often, when we are grieving, we may feel very alone. We may feel as if we are the only one in the world who has felt the pain of losing someone we love. While every person's experience with death and grief is very individual, we all share some common things in our experiences. We all miss the ones we love who have died, we all hurt inside. We all have times that we feel pain. Others who have experienced grief can understand those feelings. When we communicate about our feelings and experiences in grief, we can discover that we are not alone in our experiences. The feeling that someone else understands our feelings and experiences in grief can help us to feel supported and encouraged. We can know we are not alone.

Feelings Chart

A good way to communicate your feelings to people who love and support you is to have a feelings chart. You can fill in the chart anytime you want. You can make your chart on a large poster board or keep your chart in a small notebook, journal, or calendar. You can also use only written words if you choose, like this:

Today I feel: _____

Or, if you want to communicate your feelings more than one time a day:

Right now, I feel: _____

Some people like to use pictures. These might be actual photographs of different facial expressions depicting many different feelings. You could have someone take photos of yourself, making different facial expressions, or you could find pictures of other people, in magazines or online, that you print out to create your feelings chart. You may choose to use pictures that you or someone else has drawn. Many pre-made feelings charts are available to purchase online and in teaching stores.

To make your own photographic feelings chart, write a list of different feelings. Try to include all the feelings you think you might have at any given time. If you have trouble, you can use some or all of the feelings from the following lists.

✓

Pleasant Feelings

happy	content	excited	grateful
interested	curious	satisfied	optimistic
important	proud	confident	loving
cheerful	considerate	inspired	loved
relaxed	sympathetic	great	healthy
kind	playful	energetic	festive
sweet	interesting	skillful	thrilled
peaceful	joyful	eager	clever
hopeful	lucky	unique	certain
pretty	bright	secure	glad
calm	affectionate	certain	at ease
surprised	comfortable	strong	brave
pleased	exceptional	fearless	brilliant

Unpleasant Feelings

sad	worried	edgy	lost
lonely	annoyed	bored	upset
nervous	depressed	impatient	embarrassed
hurt	angry	ugly	aggressive
unpleasant	insulted	resentful	enraged
scared	tearful	heartbroken	dull
disgusted	hopeless	alone	powerless
anxious	guilty	jumpy	afraid
grumpy	helpless	mad	useless
frustrated	scared	jealous	ashamed
terrible	doubtful	stress	empty
disappointed	clumsy	irritable	confused
cross	distressed	troubled	hopeless

✓

Neutral Feelings

shy	quiet	neutral	uninterested
still	resting	satisfactory	adequate
okay	fine	alert	well
lazy	impartial	agreeable	tolerant

Body Feelings/Signals

hungry	thirsty	sore	tired
exhausted	overloaded	sleepy	hot
weak	hurt	in pain	ill
sick	cold	achy	stressed

Any Other Feelings You Can Think Of:

. . . .

. . . .

. . . .

. . . .

. . . .

✓

Here is a very simply drawn feelings chart. You can use it anytime you wish or use it as a guide to create your own. If you like, you can photocopy it, laminate it, and use a dry erase pen to circle your feeling. You can do that with your own feelings chart as well. You can draw your own feeling onto the blank face, or write how you might be feeling, if your feeling is different from any of the feelings pictured in the series of faces.

Figure 7.1 Feelings Chart.

Chapter 8

We Can Always Remember the People We Love Who Have Died

We can always remember the people we love who have died.
We can tell other people about them.
We can talk about the fun things we did, the games we played, or the places we visited.
We can look at pictures of them and pictures of us together when they were alive.

Remember that it is okay to talk about the ones we love who have died. When others talk about the people in their lives whom they love, and you think about the one you love who has died, you can speak up, join the conversation, and mention your loved one if you want to. Sometimes others may be uncomfortable talking about people who have died, but this is okay. It is very hard for many people to think about and talk about death. This does not mean that we should not talk about it anyway. It is okay to talk about the people we love who have died. You can decide *who* you do and do not want to talk to about the one you love who died. You can decide *when* you do or don't want to talk about your loved one. If someone is uncomfortable or upset about you wanting to talk about your loved one, you might want to share this book with them, or even some of your drawings or parts of your journal. It's up to you. You can decide.

There are other ways that we can remember our loved ones who have died. We can create things, plant things, write things, cook things. The rest of this chapter and the next chapter discuss and share ways to remember the people we love who have died by doing many different kinds of activities. You can do the activities in the chapters, or use them as guides to create your own ways to remember your loved one.

Make a Memory Box

You can create a memory box to hold the special things that remind you of your loved one. You can do this with an adult or by yourself, with help from an adult when you need it.

To make your box you will need:

- An empty box with a lid. You can choose any sort of box that you like, as long as it has a lid that can be removed or flipped up to allow you easy access inside. Some people might like a bigger box, like a hat box. Some might like a smaller box, like a cigar box. You can choose a wooden box or an already made **papier mâché** box from a crafts store. Pre-made papier mâché boxes come in all sorts of different sizes and shapes. You might also like a shoebox you already have in your closet, or another box you find somewhere else. Be sure to ask permission before you use a box you find elsewhere. You might also want to ask an adult to take you to an antiques shop or a thrift store to search for old jewelry boxes. Choose a box that feels right to you.

- Glue, or a **decoupage** medium, or acrylic gel medium (ask for this at a crafts store).

- Paint, markers, colored papers—like construction paper, wrapping paper, tissue paper; photos or pictures cut from magazines or printed out from the internet, words or letters you've cut out, fabric, ribbon, anything you like that can be smoothed, drawn, glued or painted onto a flat surface. You can use any combination of these kinds of things to decorate the outside and inside of your memory box.

- Different decorative items like buttons or beads, stickers, glitter, sequins, or anything you like that you can glue to the box. Make sure you don't choose anything too heavy that might fall off.

- Optional: **varnish** or **shellac** for making your box shiny and adding a nice finish when you have finished decorating it.

When you begin to make your box, it is important to remember that there is no one way to make a memory box. You may want to begin by painting your box any color you like and then adding other things to the box, like photos, glitter, stickers, or writing. You can cover your box with paper or use the decoupage method of placing and gluing different pieces of paper or photos onto a surface and sealing it with varnish, shellac, or a decoupage medium. You can decorate only the outside, or you can decorate and finish the inside as well. How you decide to make and decorate your box is completely up to you.

When your box is finished, you can keep special things inside it that remind you of your loved one. You can put your poems, journal entries, or art work inside the box. You might also put special things that you have that once belonged to your loved one, like a watch or other piece of jewelry, a pen they wrote with, a card or letter they sent you, a piece of their clothing. If the box is too small for a whole piece of clothing, you could ask an adult to cut a piece of their clothing and give you the piece of material. You can also make a **sachet** out of a piece of material that came from an article of clothing your loved one wore. (Read how to make a sachet in the next project.) You might want to include pictures of your loved one, or a picture of the two of you together. You can put cards or letters they gave you when they were alive, or letters that you write to them now that they have died. Keep anything you like in your special memory box.

Figure 8.1 Memory box examples by the author.

Figure 8.2 A decoupaged memory box by 11-year-old Bentley Mescall, made after her cousin Jake died. Also pictured is a matching memory journal to keep inside the box.

Make a Sachet

To make your sachet you will need:

- A piece of fabric that you like, or that reminds you of your loved one. You might also choose to use a handkerchief or a piece of clothing that belonged to your loved one. Make sure it is okay to cut up whatever piece of clothing or fabric you choose.

- A dinner plate (8", 10" or 12" [20cm, 25cm or 30cm] in diameter), if you want to use a circular piece of fabric.

- A pencil or fabric marker.

- A pair of scissors.

- Dried flowers *or* cotton balls scented with fragrance or scented oil (see instructions below for more information on this).

- Piece of yarn or ribbon of your choice.

- Optional: sewing supplies (needle, thread).

- Optional: **pinking shears**.

- Optional: anti-fray fabric glue.

Figure 8.3 Supplies you will need to create your sachet.

To make your sachet:

1. Ask an adult for permission and help to choose a piece of fabric, clothing, or a handkerchief that belonged to your loved one. The piece of clothing should be something that can be cut up.

2. Using a dinner plate as a guide, draw a circle in pencil or fabric marker around the plate.

3. Cut out the circle with a sturdy pair of scissors. You may need to ask for help with the scissors.

If you choose to use a handkerchief that belonged to your loved one, there is no need to cut. This will give you a square shape to work with. If you like squares better than circles, you can also cut a square shape from the piece of clothing you have chosen to use for your sachet. A 12"x 12" (30cm x 30cm) square may work best. Once you have cut your shape, you can leave the edges as they are if you like. If you know how to sew, sew around the edge of the fabric using a whip stitch, or get some anti-fray glue from a fabric store. You can also ask an adult who sews to help you. Cutting your fabric with pinking shears will help the fabric to be resistant to fraying.

Figure 8.4 Drawing the circle onto fabric, using a dinner plate as a guide.

4. When you decide that your circle or square is finished, place in the center of it a small amount of dried, scented flowers, or some cotton balls sprayed with a fragrance that reminds you of your loved one.

You may also choose a scent that makes you feel calm or peaceful. If your loved one wore a special fragrance, or loved a certain smell, you may want to scent your sachet with his or her favorite scent.

5. Gather the edges of the fabric around your scented flowers or cotton balls and tie tightly with a piece of yarn or ribbon.

Figure 8.5 Placing dried lavender flowers in the center of the sachet fabric. This example shows the use of a handkerchief for the sachet.

You can put the sachet in a drawer to scent your clothes, put it under your pillow, in your memory box, or any other special place you like. You may even want to carry it with you for a while.

If you are sensitive to smells and do not like scented things, you may simply wish to make a small pillow or a scentless sachet from your loved one's clothing or handkerchief. You can also simply carry the piece of material with you, place it in your memory box or keep it wherever you wish.

Figure 8.6 Finished sachets, one made from a circle of fabric cut from a skirt, the other from a handkerchief.

Make a Collage

You have probably made collages in school, in an art class, or just for fun. "Collage" is from a word in the French language meaning "to paste." The French word is *coller*. Making a collage when you are grieving the death of someone you love can be a very helpful thing to do. It can help you to know more about your feelings and can help you feel connected to the one you love who has died. You can make a collage on your own or you can make collages with friends or with family as a group project.

To make your collage you will need:

- heavy poster board, a large piece of cardboard, or another sturdy, flat surface that will hold your collaged pieces and your glue

- pictures and images from magazines or the internet

- photos of your loved one

- shoebox, envelope, or other container in which to store your cut-out images

- A pair of scissors

- glue or acrylic gel medium

- glitter, ribbon, yarn, colored or patterned paper, fabric, stickers, stamps, rhinestones, sequins, small seashells, anything you like that you would want to use in your collage.

Ask an adult to help you find old magazines that are okay to cut up. Ask your librarian, school, doctor's office, dentist's office, salon, etc. about saving their old magazines for your collage projects. Search through the magazines for pictures and words that remind you of your loved one, or you may look for anything that stands out or creates a strong feeling inside you. It does not matter if you don't understand why certain pictures or words might stand out to you. If you see it and it attracts your attention or creates a feeling inside you, even a feeling you can't name, cut it out. You can cut out as many pictures and words as you like. Spend as much time cutting out things as you like.

Once you feel as though you have enough pictures and words, then you are ready to start your collage. To begin, spread all your pictures and words out and choose the ones you want for your collage. Search through your collection for particular images or words that stand out right now. Gather several images and begin to place those images onto your base. When you find a placement design that pleases you, speaks to you, or feels right, then begin to glue them into place. You can continue to add more pictures and images or words if you choose. Keep placing and gluing your pictures, images, and words until you feel you are finished. You can make more than one collage if you want to. When you are finished gluing on your pictures and words and photographs (if you choose to use them), you can then add other things like glitter, rhinestones, stickers, ribbon—anything you feel is right and that your glue will hold. There is no right or wrong way to make your collage.

Your collage may be something you want to keep private, or you may want to share it with other family or friends. You may choose to hang your collage as a memorial to your loved one or as a reminder of your own feelings. The pictures and words you have chosen and how you have decided to put them together are a picture of how you are feeling inside. You might want to spend time thinking about this or you may choose to write a poem or story or your private thoughts in your journal.

Figure 8.7 Example of collage created by the author's husband, Jamie Fueglein. This collage was made from different cut-out pictures of flowers surrounding our son Theo's face.

Chapter 9

We Will Always
Miss Them

We will always miss them.
We will always love them.
It's okay to be sad sometimes.
It's okay to cry sometimes.
But we can be happy too, and it's okay!

You can have all kinds of feelings when you are grieving. You should know that the death of someone you love is not something you will ever "get over." You will not always feel as sad as you may feel now, but you will never forget that person who means so much to you. And you should not have to. It is okay to remember those people who mean so much. The person you love who has died can never be replaced. It only makes sense that when they are gone from your life, it hurts inside and you will miss them, no matter how long they have been gone. There are days that you will feel sad, and that you may cry, maybe even years after the one you love has died. But there will be many, many days that you will feel better and that you will be happy. This is okay. Your loved one would want you to feel happy.

There will be times in your life when it is harder to be without them than at other times. There will be special days like the person's birthday, even your own birthday, because this person you love will not be there to share it with you. Holidays and other special days, like the anniversary of the day they died, will be harder than other, more ordinary days. This is okay. You will be okay. Make a plan for some way to remember and honor the one who has died on these special days. As described in Chapter 4, create your own ritual of remembering. Talk to someone you trust, a family member or a friend, who can help you. Other people in your life may be missing this special person too, and they may want to join in remembering the one that you love.

Some Suggestions for Ways to Remember the One You Love

Many of these activities should be done with the help of a trusted adult. You can do some of them alone. Some would be good to do with your whole family, especially if other people in your family are also missing this special person. Family rituals and memorial activities are good to do on holidays, on your loved one's birthday or death anniversary, or on days that are special for other reasons. It is good to do things to remember loved ones who have died, by yourself as well as with others who love them too. When you do these things with others you love and trust, you can also feel more loved and supported. Feeling loved and supported when you are grieving is very important.

- **Ask an adult to help you light a candle.** The lighting of a candle is a symbol for many things. The flame of the candle can be thought to represent your love for the person who has died, continuing to burn bright. The flame of a candle represents bringing light to darkness. Sometimes when we are grieving, we can feel as though we are in darkness. Lighting a candle can bring some comfort by helping us feel we are bringing some light to the darkness. The flame can also represent the life of the person when they were alive. It can represent their love for you and your love for them. Even when the candle is burned or blown out, that love still exists. By lighting a candle, you are acknowledging this love. You can decide what lighting a candle means to you.

You can choose to light a candle to remember your loved one at any time. You can light a candle when you are feeling sad or especially missing your loved one. You may also choose to light a candle at specific or special times. For example, you might choose dinner time, or on a certain day of the week, or you might choose to light a candle on extra special days like holidays and anniversaries.

- **Set an extra plate at the table** during holiday or family gatherings, or at other special times, to represent your loved one. You might ask each person at the table to tell a favorite memory about your loved one.

- **Create a scrapbook** and fill it with photographs, cards, letters, or other things you have saved that remind you of your loved one.

- **Spend time listening to your loved one's favorite music.**

- **Watch his or her favorite movie.**

- **Create a special CD or playlist of music** that reminds you of your loved one and listen to it on special days, or anytime you want to remember.

- **Plant a tree or flowers** in your loved one's memory.

- **Ask an adult about helping you raise some money to make a donation to a charity** that your loved one supported, or a charity that reminds you of your loved one.

- **Go and visit your loved one's burial site.**

- **Carry something special with you that reminds you of your loved one.** Take it out and hold it when you need to. This might be a piece of jewelry, something your loved one gave you, something that belonged to them, or something that reminds you of a special time.

- **Create a work of art in your loved one's memory.**

    - **Cook a special meal in honor of your loved one.** This is good to do any time, but especially on your loved one's birthday or another special day that you choose.

    - **Sing a song, make up a dance, or write a special poem or story** dedicated especially to your loved one. You can keep this private or you can share it with others.

    - **Follow or create activities in the style of rituals of other cultures.**

Some Customs From Other Countries and Cultures That You May Find Interesting and Inspiring

Japan

The Japanese celebrate a holiday called *Obon* to honor the spirits of departed **ancestors**. *Obon* lasts for three days and usually occurs in the middle of July. Over those three days, many families have reunions and family dinners. They participate in many rituals and festival activities, including carnivals with rides and games, as they celebrate the lives of their loved ones who have died. Traditionally, foods served at the festivals are summertime treats such as watermelon and ice cream.

Part of the festivals include elaborate dances called ***Bon Odori***, originally meant to welcome the spirits of the dead. Each region of Japan has different types of dances with different types of music.

The *Obon* festival traditionally ends on the third day with the festival of ***Toro nagashi***, the "Festival of Floating Lanterns" in which families float decorated paper lanterns down a river or on the ocean. The tradition is based on the belief that the lanterns help to guide the spirits of their ancestors back to the other world where they reside after death.

To celebrate *Obon*, you may wish to invite your family members friends to come to a festival dinner where you can serve special summertime festival foods such as fruits, ice cream, foods cooked on a grill, or serve your loved one's favorite summertime foods. For your *Obon* festivities, you may also wish to try the following activities.

Create your own *Bon Odori*

You can create your own dance to honor the memory of your loved one. You may choose to create a dance to the music of one of your loved one's favorite songs, or create your own music with instruments you have available. You may also choose to dance silently, with no music at all. In Japan, the *Bon Odori* is a often performed as a group dance, practiced for weeks before the festivals begin. To make your *Bon Odori* a group activity, you can ask friends and family to participate. You may want to plan and practice your dance ahead of time, or teach different parts of the dance to friends and family members. Another choice would be to do an improvised dance, making up dance movements as you hear the music playing. You may also choose to create a dance to honor your loved one at any time of the year. You can do this in private or you can share your dance with someone you trust.

Make your own *Toro nagashi*

Another way to celebrate *Obon* is to create your own *Toro nagashi*, a floating paper lantern, to honor your loved one. After the lantern is made, you may choose to float it on a small pool in your own back yard, in a birdbath, or in any other body of water. If you float the lantern in a large pond, lake, or river and want to keep it, be sure to securely attach a string or rope to the lantern, so that you can bring it back to you. If you float your lantern in a public place, be certain that there are no rules or laws preventing you from floating objects on the water.

To make a Toro nagashi *you will need:*

- YUPO® translucent taper or vellum crafting paper. You will need one 9" × 12" (23cm × 30cm) sheet per lantern, or you can cut a sheet in half for smaller lanterns. "Translucent" means that light can pass through easily.

  - YUPO® translucent paper is a special kind of synthetic paper that is similar to very thin plastic, but which can be painted or drawn on. It will not be harmed by water if you do float your lantern and it will be very strong and longlasting.

  - Vellum is a type of paper that was once made from animal skin and was one of the first writing surfaces ever created. Many historical documents were recorded on vellum and still exist today. Vellum is now made from wood and vegetable fibers. It is stronger than regular paper and is also translucent.

- Markers or paints to decorate your lantern. If you are going to use your lantern outdoors, or float it on water, use waterproof paints or markers.

- Brushes for paint if you choose to use paint.

- A pair of scissors for cutting your paper as needed.

- A light source for your lantern to glow. The safest way to illuminate your lantern is with a small battery-operated candle with a low-wattage bulb. Tealight candles placed inside a 2" (5cm) high votive holder are the best choice for safety when using real candles. This will ensure that the sides of your lantern do not touch the candle. If you do use a real candle, make sure you have permission to do so, and if necessary, allow a grown-up to light the candle for you.

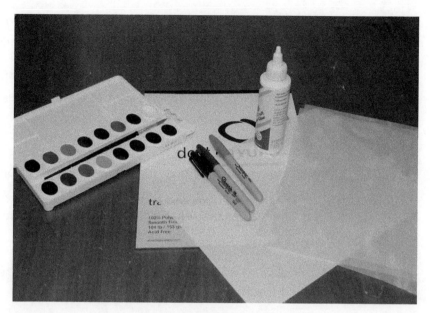

Figure 9.1 Supplies you will need to make your *Toro nagashi*.

To preserve the environment and take care of our planet, you should not float your lantern on a body of water that will carry your creation away. You can choose to attach a string to your lantern so that you can retrieve it. This could be done with a staple. You can also choose to float it on a small pond, or even in a swimming pool. You could even choose to float it in a bathtub if you wish! If you choose to float your lantern, make sure you have permission to do so.

To make your Toro nagashi*:*

1. If you choose, you can make your drawings on a separate sheet of paper. The transparency of the YUPO® or vellum allows you to place a drawing you have made ahead of time beneath the lantern paper for tracing.

2. Decorate your paper with your drawing or painting. If you choose to use paint, remember that the YUPO® paper or vellum won't absorb your paints in the same way regular paper does. The paints will remain more fluid on the surface and drying time may be increased. Also, fingerprints on the

surface of your papers may leave oils that disrupt the paint or ink coverage, so make sure you have clean, dry hands.

3. Fold or roll the lantern, leaving about a half inch (1cm) for glue. See Figures 9.2 through 9.8 for the folding pattern to create a rectangular lantern. For a round lantern, simply roll your paper to create a tube.

4. Place a small amount of glue on one edge of the paper to join the edges. Use a paper clip to secure the seam while it dries. Remember that glue will show through translucent paper once the lantern is lit.

5. After the glue has dried, you can choose the type of base you would like to use.

How to crease your paper for a rectangular lantern

Figure 9.2 Create a ½" (1cm) crease at the bottom of the paper.

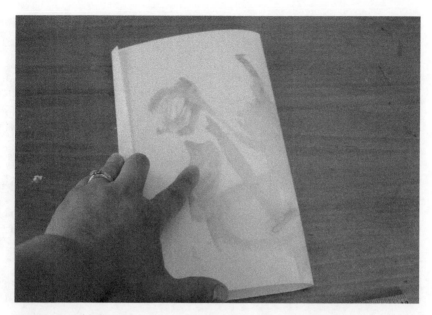

Figure 9.3 Fold the paper over so that the other edge of it meets the crease you made at the bottom. Unfold.

Figure 9.4 This creates a crease in the center of the paper.

Figure 9.5 Fold the edge of the paper over again, to meet the center crease you just made.

Figure 9.6 Fold it again to meet the initial ½" (1cm) crease you made when you began folding the edges.

Figure 9.7 Unfolded, it should look like this.

Figure 9.8 Standing, it should look like this.

Making a base for your lantern:

Non-floating bases can be paper plates or small dishes. You can fill the inside of the lantern with about 2½" (5cm) of sand or pebbles to weight it down. You can place your light source on the sand or pebbles. You can also use transparent tape to attach the lantern to the base from the inside, but remember that the tape will show through when you light your lantern.

Floating bases can be created from a block of wood or bamboo, or you can easily make a waterproof floating base with another piece of YUPO® paper or vellum.

To make a waterproof floating base for your lantern using YUPO® paper or vellum:

1. Cut a sheet of YUPO® paper or vellum into 4.5" × 6" (12.5cm × 15cm) pieces. One piece of 9" × 12" (23cm × 30cm) paper will make 4 squares per sheet.

2. Make ½" inch [1cm] creases on all four sides of the piece of paper.

Figure 9.9 A 4.5" × 6" (12.5cm × 15cm) piece of YUPO® paper creased ½" (1cm) on all four sides.

3. Fold each corner upward slightly, toward the center of the piece of paper. Pinch each corner into an inward fold.

Figure 9.10 Pinching the corners inward.

Figure 9.11 Finished lanterns.

Source: This activity was gratefully adapted from Dick Blick Art Materials® Japanese Floating Lanterns Lesson.

China

The Chinese holiday **Teng Chieh** is held at the end of the Chinese New Year festivities, on the full moon following the New Year. It marks the day when Chinese people traditionally believe that the spirits of ancestors and others they love who have died come to visit and mingle with their families and loved ones. They light many lanterns, very similar to the tradition of the Japanese *Obon* festival, except the Chinese lanterns are not all set on the water. They also light huge **bonfires**. They believe the lanterns and the bonfires will help the spirits see the way to their loved ones. During *Teng Chieh*, families place bowls of food and water in front of photographs of their loved ones who have died. The festival is sometimes called "The Feast of Hungry Ghosts" because the belief is that the spirits have travelled very far so that they must be thirsty and hungry once they finally arrive! The Chinese New Year is focused on family and togetherness. Each member of the family continues to be important, even after they have died.

The Chinese have another festival day called **Qingming**, or *Ching Ming*, which is held on the fifteenth day following the Spring Equinox, about two weeks after the first day of spring. The festival name can be translated as "Clear Bright Festival" and it is also called "Ancestors' Day" or "Tomb-Sweeping Day." On this day, families gather together to visit the burial places of those they love who have died. They take picnic foods and spend the day together, cleaning and tidying up the burial places of their loved ones. They place food at the graves and pour **libations** of wine and other drinks onto the ground where their loved ones are buried. Another tradition is to bring willow branches to the gravesites of loved ones. Each family member has the opportunity to bow to their ancestors and to communicate with them, each in their own way.

Other popular things to do on *Qingming* are to go for walks in the woods or across meadows, to begin spring planting and plowing, and to fly kites. Families often buy or make kites in the shapes of animals and fly them at the burial sites.

Kite Flying

You can go ask permission to purchase a kite and fly it with someone who can help you. Everyone in the family can have his or her own kite if they like! The Chinese tradition is to fly kites in the shapes of animals, but you can choose any kind of kite you like. You may even want to personalize your kite by writing your loved one's name on the kite, or drawing a picture in their memory onto the kite. There are also several do-it-yourself kite kits that can be purchased in most crafts stores, some toy stores, and online.

When a windy, breezy spring day comes, your kite will be ready to take off and fly on the breeze! You can imagine your loved one being able to see the colorful designs you drew in his or her memory, all the while your kite is flying.

Mexico

The Mexican holiday known as *El Dia De Los Muertos*, or **Day of the Dead**, is celebrated on November 1st and 2nd each year. Babies and children who have died are honored on the first day. This day is known as *El Dia de los Inocentes* or *El Dia de los Angelitos*, **Day of the Innocents** or **Day of the Little Angels**. Adults who have died are honored on November 2nd.

During Day of the Dead festivities, families spend time building and placing traditional items, or **ofrenda**, on their home altars. They spend time remembering, talking, and telling stories about their loved ones who have died, and they do a lot of cooking and eat special meals together. On the afternoon of November 2nd they take a special trip to the places where their loved ones are buried, to clean and decorate the burial place. Often, families will spend all afternoon and into the late evenings cleaning, decorating, having picnics, and then lighting candles and telling stories about the ones they love who have died. The holiday is a fun, happy time meant to celebrate the lives of those who have died and to be thankful for having had them in the life of the family. The traditional symbols for Day of the Dead are skulls called **calaveras**, and whimsical skeleton sculptures called **calacas**. The *calaveras* and *calacas* are usually represented in handmade crafts, paintings, drawings, and small sculptures. They are typically dressed in bright colors and the *calacas* are usually depicted as having fun, dancing, playing musical instruments, and taking part in the celebration of life. Part of the meaning of the holiday is also to help people to remember that death is a part of life and that life is to be celebrated.

The holiday is celebrated all over Mexico and many places in the United States, as well as in other countries. There are many festivals and functions all over the world which highlight the crafts and food of the Day of the Dead celebrations. There are many Day of the Dead traditions you can take part in. You may choose to make **sugar skulls**—traditional sculptures shaped like skulls and made of sugar and meringue. The sugar mixture is pressed into skull-shaped molds, allowed to harden, and then decorated with bright, colorful icing and other decorations. You can make all kinds of crafts, drawings, paintings, or clay sculptures in the style of Day of the Dead crafts with a skeleton theme. You can bake the traditional bread called ***pan de muerto***. You and your family may even choose to have a Day of the Dead party, inviting others to come to your home to help honor the memory of your loved ones, as well as their own!

Some suggestions you may wish to follow if you decide to have a Day of the Dead party

- Have your party on or near the dates of the traditional festivities, November 1st or 2nd. The weekends before or after are also okay. The ancient festival was first celebrated by the Aztec people and lasted for an entire month!

- Have your favorite Mexican foods, like tacos, nachos or quesadillas, along with some of your loved one's favorite foods.

- Make sugar cookies rolled and cut out with skull-shaped cookie cutters. Bake and decorate them with brightly colored icing and sprinkles.

- Bake some *pan de muerto,* or "bread of the dead," the traditional sweet bread made on the holiday, to share with family and friends.

- Set up an **altar,** or *ofrenda,* in your home in the traditional Mexican style. These are the traditional elements of a Day of the Dead altar:

  ○ a colorful cloth to cover the surface of the altar space

  ○ pictures of your loved one

  ○ flowers (traditionally marigolds are used)

  ○ small items or **mementos** that represent your loved one. These might be actual things that belonged to your loved one, things that remind you of your loved one, or things you think your loved one would like or enjoy

  ○ skull and skeleton decorations, like the traditional sugar skulls or other colorful skeleton crafts

  ○ dishes of your loved one's favorite foods, or traditional foods of the holiday.

- Day of the Dead altars often include incense or candles and a bowl of salt. Salt is often referred to as the "spice of life."

An altar can be dedicated to one person in particular, or you may want to have a family altar to honor several loved ones who have died. Even relatives and ancestors who died many years ago can be honored on the Day of the Dead.

If you have a Day of the Dead party, you may want to make a group altar by covering a table with a brightly colored cloth. Add flowers, candles and incense. Ask guests to bring photos of those they love who have died. Add the photos of your loved ones who have died and include the ones your guests bring. You may want to add other mementos or objects that remind you of your loved ones. Add a dish or two of the foods you have prepared for the party, and some traditional skeleton decorations or other crafts you may have made to honor your loved ones.

Even if you don't have a party, you can still try some of the traditions to celebrate the Day of the Dead. Homemade food and decorations are an important part of the celebrations of Day of the Dead.

Make your own whimsical skeletons or *calacas*

To make these calacas, *you will need:*

- white pipe cleaners or chenille stems

- white air dryable modeling compound, such as Model Magic® or Amaco Cloud Clay

- black, and other brightly colored, fine-tipped permanent markers

- brightly colored pieces of felt or other fabric to make hats, dresses, scarves or other clothing.

Figure 9.12 Supplies to make your *calacas.*

To make your whimsical calacas:

1. Bend and twist two or three pipe cleaners into a shape of a body with arms, legs, neck, and head. You can bend the pieces back onto themselves, creating a double layer. This step does not have to be perfect. You will be covering this frame with your air-drying clay.

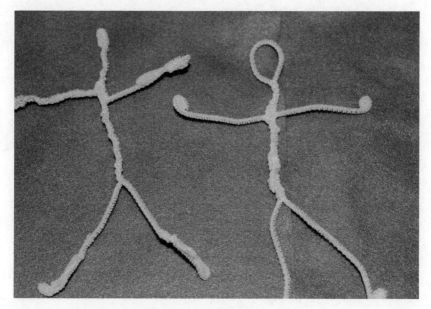

Figure 9.13 Examples of different *calacas* frames.

2. Take chunks of air-drying clay into your hands, squeezing them into the approximate sizes and shapes of your skeleton frame. Cover your pipe cleaner frame with clay. Remember that the body does not need to look like a real skeleton at all.

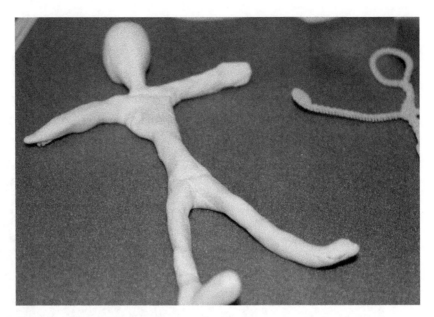

Figure 9.14 Pipe cleaner frame covered with clay.

3. Once your skeleton is covered with white air-drying clay, follow the instructions for your choice of clay for drying time.

4. After your skeleton is dry, use fine-tipped markers to draw a skeleton face—eye holes, nose hole, teeth, outline of skull and cheekbones—and outlines for the bones of the body.

5. You can use brightly colored fine-tipped markers to draw flowers, hearts, or other shapes onto the faces of the *calacas*.

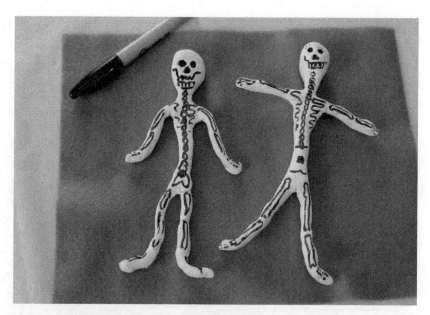

Figure 9.15 Outlines of skeletons on the *calacas*.

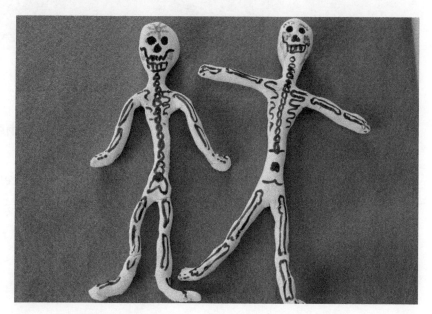

Figure 9.16 Designs drawn onto the *calacas* with colored markers.

6. If you want to make clothes for your *calacas*, use brightly colored felt and cut out simple shapes for skirts, pants, scarves or hats. You can use fabric glue to attach the clothing to your *calacas*.

Figure 9.17 Finished *calacas*!

Make your own *pan de muerto* or "bread of the dead"

Remember to have a trusted adult help with cooking if needed. Making *pan de muerto* can be a very good thing to do with other people. Below is the recipe.

Ingredients:

- ¼ cup margarine

- ¼ cup milk

- ¼ cup warm water (110°F/45°C)

- 3 cups all-purpose flour

- 1 ¼ teaspoons active dry yeast

  - ½ teaspoon salt

  - 2 teaspoons anise seed

  - ¼ cup white sugar

  - 2 eggs, beaten

  - 2 teaspoons orange zest (zest is a food ingredient made by scraping the colorful outer skin of citrus fruits like oranges, lemons, and limes).

For the glaze:

  - ¼ cup white sugar

  - ¼ cup orange juice

  - 1 tablespoon orange zest

  - 2 tablespoons white sugar for sprinkling on top of glazed bread.

Figure 9.18 Ingredients for *pan de muerto*.

To make your bread:

1. Heat the milk and the butter together in a medium-sized saucepan, until the butter melts. Remove from the heat and add the ¼ cup of warm water.

2. In a large bowl combine 1 cup of the flour, the yeast, salt, the anise seed and the ¼ cup of sugar. Beat in the warm milk mixture, then add the eggs and orange zest if you are using it, and beat until well combined. Stir in a ½ cup of the flour, and then continue adding more flour a bit at a time until the dough is soft and beginning to pull away from the sides of your mixing bowl.

3. Turn the dough out onto a lightly floured surface and knead the dough until it is smooth and elastic, about 9–10 minutes.

Figure 9.19 Step 2: Mixing the dough.

Figure 9.20 Step 3: Kneading the dough.

4. Place the dough into a lightly greased bowl. Cover with plastic wrap and let rise in a warm place until it is doubled in size.

5. Punch down the dough, turn out onto a floured surface and knead again, briefly. Divide the dough into two pieces. Shape one piece into a round loaf. Divide the other piece into three smaller pieces. Shape one of these into a skull-type shape and two into bone-shaped pieces. Place the round loaf onto a baking sheet, then arrange your skull and bone pieces on top of the round loaf. Loosely cover the whole thing with plastic wrap and let rise again in a warm place for about 1 hour or until just about doubled in size.

6. Bake in a preheated 350°F (175°C) oven for about 35–45 minutes. Remove from oven, let cool slightly, then brush with glaze.

Figure 9.21 Placing the bread into the oven.

7. Make glaze: In a small saucepan combine ¼ cup sugar, orange juice and orange zest. Bring to a boil over medium heat and boil for two minutes. Remove from heat and brush over top of bread while it is still warm.

Figure 9.22 Brushing the bread with glaze.

8. Sprinkle glazed bread with white or colored sugar.

9. Enjoy!

Haiti

The Haitian celebration of the Festival **Ghede** (pronounced GEH-day) is similar to Mexico's Day of the Dead, and is also celebrated on 2 November each year. In Haiti, as in Mexico, many of the people practice the Catholic religion. A great many of Catholic people there also practice beliefs from a religion called *Voudon*, sometimes called "Voodoo." *Voudon* is a mixture of customs and beliefs from the Catholic religion and customs and beliefs which African people brought with them to the island of Haiti many years ago. During this festival day, families prepare for a religious ritual during which they pray to a deity known as **Baron Samedi**, who is the ruler of death in the *Voudon* religion, and who is also thought to be the protector of children and the hope for a cure or healing for many people, children and adults, who are very ill. During the festival of *Ghede*, many people dress in the colors of Baron Samedi, purple, white and black, and they may also paint their faces white. Once they are dressed, people visit cemeteries, where families clean the burial places of their loved ones. Many people pray, drummers drum and singers sing. Thousands of people go to cemeteries to participate in the *Ghede* celebrations.

Similar to the Mexican Day of the Dead *ofrendas*, Haitian families also construct altars for the special day. Altars are built to honor Baron Samedi and his role in taking spirits of loved ones to the spirit world. He is always pictured with a top hat and a cane, and often with a white face, or the face of a skull. Representations of Baron Samedi's top hat and cane are almost always part of the altars dedicated to him. Families spend a lot of time cooking and making great feasts in honor of their loved ones and ancestors, usually with traditional foods special to each family. They decorate **shrines** and memorials dedicated to their loved ones and have special ceremonies when they light candles, pray, and call out the names of their ancestors and loved ones.

I hope that you have now gotten some ideas of ways to remember and honor your loved one. You may choose to sing a song, create a dance, have a party, place flowers in front of a photograph, write a letter, light a candle, or make up your own special way to express your feelings.

It is important to remember that each one of us grieves and expresses our grief, and all of our feelings, in different ways. I encourage you to find your own way of remembering the ones you love who have died. I also encourage you to find your own special ways of expressing your feelings. To learn more about grief and ways to help yourself feel better, visit some of the websites listed in the resources section of this book.

Glossary

afterlife: A life or an existence believed by some to continue after physical death.

altar: Usually a raised structure on which offerings are made or religious actions are performed in church, temple, synagogue, or other place of worship. Some families have home altars as well, where they may burn candles or incense and place offerings or objects that are connected to religion or a spiritual practice. Sometimes family members may pray or meditate at a family altar.

ancestors: People from whom you are descended—usually meaning those family members who lived and died long ago, in the time before your great-grandparents, grandparents, and parents.

anniversary: The date on which an event took place in previous years, such as a birth, marriage, or death.

Autism, Autism Spectrum Disorders (ASD): Autism is a group of developmental disorders collectively known as "Autism Spectrum Disorders." ASD refers to the first three letters of Autism Spectrum Disorder. It is called a spectrum of disorders because of the wide range of skills, abilities and/or impairments a person with ASD can display, or not display. Some people may be mildly affected by symptoms of autism, some people may be more severely affected.

Baron Samedi: A *loa*, or spirit, of the Haitian religion, *Vodoun*. He is the spirit of the dead, usually shown wearing a top hat and tuxedo, and with a white skull face. He is the spirit who is thought to greet the spirits of those who have died and guide them to the afterlife.

belief system: A set of beliefs, usually involving religion, that is shared in certain areas of the world or in certain communities. A belief system can also be a *personal* set of beliefs that a person, family, or other group of people consciously chooses for themselves to believe in.

bereavement: A state of feeling deprived of someone or something after a loss or death.

bonfire: A large fire, lit outdoors, usually as part of a celebration, to mark an occasion or to send signals.

bon odori: A style of dancing performed during the Japanese festival of *Obon*. Each region of Japan has a local dance style. Originally the *bon odori* was danced to welcome the spirits of the dead during *Obon*.

burial: The practice of placing the body of someone who has died into a grave that has been dug in the ground, or a **mausoleum**.

butcher's paper: Large, wide roll of strong paper that can be used to wrap food, cover surfaces, or for art making. Butcher's paper is available in most office supply and arts and crafts stores.

calaca: A sort of slang Mexican Spanish word (or idiom) for skeleton. A *calaca* is also a usually whimsical figure of a skeleton, used for decoration and to celebrate Day of the Dead.

calavera: Spanish word for "skull."

cancer: A disease caused by the uncontrolled division and growth of abnormal cells in the body. There are many different kinds of cancer that can affect different parts of the body.

casket: A long, narrow box that a body is placed in after death. Also called a coffin.

catalyst: A person, thing or event that causes another thing to happen. There is also a chemistry definition in which a catalyst is the substance that causes a chemical change, or increases the rate of the change, without itself being affected by the chemical reaction.

celebration of life: Similar to a funeral or a memorial service, a celebration of life honors the life and memory of a person who has died. You can read more about this in Chapter 4.

cemetery: A place where the dead are buried. Some cemeteries may also have **mausoleums** where the dead may be placed above ground.

chaos: A state of disorder, confusion, and/or uncertainty.

coffin: A long, narrow box that a body is placed in after death, also called a casket.

collage: A form of art in which pieces of paper, photographs, writing, or other things are arranged and attached to a backing.

comfortable: Feeling physically and/or emotionally at ease or relaxed.

committal service: A short ritual that takes place in a graveyard, cemetery, or **mausoleum**, during which a person who has died is buried or interred. It is called a "committal service" because the person's body or remains are being "committed" to the ground or to his or her grave.

communicate: To share information, ideas, and/or feelings with others in such a way that both parties understand the messages.

cope: To manage something difficult with a fair amount of success. Coping skills are the actions and thoughts we use to deal with stressful and difficult situations.

counselor: A person who is trained to give guidance to others on social, emotional, personal, or psychological problems (see also **therapist**).

cremation: The practice of burning a dead body until it is reduced to ashes.

culture: In this book, culture is used to mean the beliefs and behaviors characteristic of, or associated with, a particular group of people.

Day of the Dead/ *El Dia de los Muertos*: Three-day Mexican holiday that celebrates and remembers loved ones who have died. It is celebrated around the world in many different cultures, beginning on 1 November.

Day of the Innocents /*El Dia de los Inocentes*: The first of the three days of *Dia de los Muertos*, which honors specifically babies and children who have died.

Day of the Little Angels /*Dia de los Angelitos*: Another name for the first day of *Dia de los Muertos*, which honors babies and children who have died.

death: The end of the life of a person, animal, plant, or other organism.

decompose: The breaking down of organic matter, which all living and dead things are made of, into smaller molecules that provide nourishment for other living things and which can make the soil fertile over time.

découpage: The craft of gluing colored papers or pictures onto an object, such a box or a tabletop.

diaphragm: A dome-shaped muscle beneath the lungs, that works with the lungs to enable a person to inhale and exhale (breathe in and out).

dictate: To say or read aloud something that is recorded or written down by another person.

emotion: A temporary state of mind that a person has as a response to a situation or circumstance. Emotions include feelings such as anger, joy, sadness, happiness, love, fear, and many others.

environment: The surroundings and conditions in which people, animals, and plants and other organisms live and carry on activities.

essence: The special quality of someone or something that makes that person or thing unique. This is usually an unseen or abstract property that cannot be measured, and without which the person or thing would not be the same.

exhale: To breathe out.

feeling/feelings: Emotional responses to situations, events or circumstances. A feeling is one particular response in a particular situation. Used as a verb, "feeling" means to be affected by a particular emotion or sensation.

funeral: A ceremony or ritual honoring a person who has died, which usually includes burial or interment of the body. You can read more about this in Chapter 4.

Ghede **(pronounced GEH-day):** *Ghede* are the family of spirits in the Haitian religion, *Voudon*, that are celebrated and communicated with on the festival of *Ghede*. The festival of *Ghede* is a day that Haitians remember their ancestors and loved ones who have died.

grateful/gratitude: A feeling people experience when they are thankful for people, things and events in our lives which make us feel happy, safe, peaceful, and good.

graveside service: A short ritual that takes place in a graveyard or cemetery, during which a person who has died is buried or interred.

graveyard: A place where the dead are buried. Some graveyards may also have **mausoleums** where the dead may be placed above ground. A graveyard and a cemetery are usually the same thing when people use those terms.

grief/grieving: The feelings experienced after someone has died or after other significant losses.

heaven: A place where, in many religions and belief systems, people believe the spirits and souls of the dead go after their bodies have died. Heaven is also a place where many people believe or imagine that religious deities and other figures live, and is associated with beliefs about the afterlife.

honor: To show evidence of respect and reverence.

hospice: A place or a program which cares for people who are dying or who have terminal illnesses. Their care focuses on making sure the person is comfortable and not in pain. Some children's hospices also care for patients who are not dying, but who have severe, chronic (ongoing) illnesses. Hospices often offer support and services for families of those who are ill.

image: A representation of a person or a thing in a picture, painting or sculpture.

individual: A single person, separate from and different from other people.

inhale: To breathe in.

interment: The burial of a dead body in a grave or a tomb.

journal: A personal record of events, occurrences, feelings, reflections, thoughts, pictures, or drawings, kept by a person on a regular basis.

libations: drinks poured out as offerings to a deity.

lifespan: The length of time that an organism lives.

mausoleum: A building that holds tombs for the bodies of the dead.

medium: The material used by an artist to create work.

memento: An object kept as a reminder of a person.

memorial service: A service or ritual honoring a person who has died, without the body present. A memorial service can happen anytime after a person has died. A memorial service usually happens much later after the death than a funeral. You can read more about this in Chapter 4.

Moksha: In the Hindu belief system, Moksha is a state of bliss and freedom that a person's spirit can reach after death.

mourn/mourning: The outward expression of feelings of grief.

natural: Present, occurring, or part of nature. "It is natural to grieve" is a way of saying that grief is a normal response to the death of someone we love.

normal: Expected, not unusual. To grieve when someone we love dies is a normal and natural response.

Obon: The Japanese festival which takes place over three days and is meant to celebrate and honor the ancestors. During the festival, families return to ancestral homes and visit family; they tend and clean graves of loved ones who have died.

ofrenda: The Spanish word for offerings.

pan de muerto: Spanish for "bread of the dead."

papier mâché: A material made from shreds of paper mixed with glue, that can be formed, shaped, sculpted, and, when dry, painted.

Paradise: Similar to Heaven, Paradise is a place where, in many religions and belief systems, people believe the spirits and souls of the dead go after their bodies have died. The belief is that there is no pain or suffering in Paradise. It is imagined to be a place of harmony and beauty.

pinking shears: Scissors with notched blades to give a zig-zag edge to cloth, or to prevent fraying.

polite: Having or showing considerate, respectful behavior.

portrait: A representation of a person, usually showing his or her face. Portraits can be done in many ways, by drawing, painting, and photography, for example.

Qingming (Ching Ming): A festival day held after the Chinese New Year, on which the Chinese people honor and remember their ancestors.

religion: A set of beliefs, behaviors, rituals, traditions and worldviews that usually involve particular thoughts about god(s)/goddess(es), and which often seek to teach moral values and/or explain the meaning of life, and reasons for humanity's existence. There are many different religions in the world. Most religions have specific behaviors, rituals, prayers, and/or practices that those who follow specific religions observe. The word "religion" is often used with the same meaning as "faith" or "belief system." Many people are brought up to believe in and practice particular religions that have been practiced in their own families or cultures.

representation: Something that depicts, shows, or describes someone or something else.

resources: Something that can be used to for help or support.

respectful: Actions or words that demonstrate polite and courteous behavior.

ritual: A ritual is an activity or a set of activities people engage in to help feel calmer, more orderly, and cope with difficult feelings. Sometimes rituals after people die are associated with religious traditions, sometimes they are not.

sachet: A small, perfumed bag usually used to scent clothing.

sensory perception: The process of experiencing, registering, recognizing, or interpreting information received through the stimulation of any of the body's senses. Senses include the traditionally known five senses—visual (seeing), auditory (hearing), tactile (touch), olfactory (smell), and taste. There are also 4 less well known senses: thermoception, the ability to detect hot and cold temperature on the skin and inside the body; nociception, the ability to detect pain or to sense damage to bodily tissue; equilibrioception, also known as the vestibular sense, the sense of balance and movement or acceleraction (whether the body is speeding up or slowing down) and is related to the fluid within the inner ear; proprioception, the sense of body awareness, knowing where the body is in space, what various parts of the body may be feeling or where and how they are moving. Many people with ASD have difficulty processing sensory information, or have extremely sensitive and highly tuned senses or both. Often people with ASD may become overwhelmed with sensory information and not know how to manage all the stimulation. This can sometimes result in "shutdown" (withdrawing, covering ears, inability to talk or engage with others), or "melt-down" (noisy outbursts, yelling, screaming, showing tantrum-like behaviors). Being and becoming more aware of how your body and brain receive and process sensory information in different kinds of situations can be very important to your well-being.

shellac: Used in this book as a verb, shellac is flakes or small pieces of lac (a substance secreted by the lac insect), dissolved in liquid and used for making varnish. "Shellac" as a verb means to cover something with shellac to impart a hard, clear, shiny surface.

shrine: A place or object of devotion or commemoration. Shrines are usually dedicated to a specific person, saint, or occurrence. A shrine can be a building, a statue, a box or case which holds objects, or pictures associated with the person to whom the shrine is dedicated. There are many different kinds of shrines. Some are dedicated to religious figures, deities and saints, and some are dedicated to people who have died.

sorrow: Deep distress or pain felt especially for the loss of someone or something greatly loved.

soul: In many belief systems, the soul is the unseen essence that animates a human body. It is also believed by many that the soul is the part of the person that lives on after the body has died.

spirit: Often used interchangeably with the word "soul." The spirit of a person is believed by many people to be the part of the person that lives on after the body is dead. Many people also believe that animals have souls or spirits too.

sugar skulls: Decoration used in the Mexican holiday "Day of the Dead." They are skulls made of a sugar mixture that has been pressed into a skull-shaped mold, allowed to dry, and then decorated with colorful icing. They are usually not eaten. They are used to symbolize the sweetness of life in the midst of the reality of death.

support: Support means "help." Support for grieving people can include providing information, listening, and comforting in whatever ways the person needs to feel comforted. There are many ways to support a person in grief.

symbol/symbolic: A symbol is something that represents or stands for something else. If you draw a picture of yourself crying, your tears in the picture could be considered symbolic of your sadness.

sympathy: The ability to share in the feelings of another, often because you have also experienced this same feeling or experience. Sympathy usually includes a desire to help the one feeling the pain.

Teng Chieh: Chinese festival which occurs at the end of the Chinese New Year on a full moon night. It marks the day when Chinese people traditionally believe that the spirits of ancestors (celebrated on **Qingming**), as well as beloved family and friends who have died recently, are able to visit and mingle with their families and loved ones.

Tian: An ancient Chinese word for "heaven" and the home of God.

tension: The state of being stretched tight.

therapist: A person trained and skilled in a type of therapy. There are many different kinds of therapists—occupational therapists, speech therapists, physical therapists, psychotherapists. Often, when talking about psychotherapists, people will shorten it to say only "therapist." Often a counselor and a therapist are the same thing. Sometimes this is not true. You can read more about the differences in the "Choosing a Therapist" section.

Toro nagashi: A Japanese floating lantern; *toro* means "lantern" and *nagashi* means "cruise or flow." The floating lanterns are traditionally used during the Japanese celebration of the festival of *Obon*.

unique: Existing as the only one of its kind, unlike anything else.

Valhalla: In ancient Norse or Viking mythology, Valhalla is the majestic hall where the god Odin receives warriors who have died in battle. Other souls also went to Valhalla. Sometimes people refer to Valhalla in modern times as a paradise or heaven.

varnish: A liquid resin, used to coat something made from wood, metal, or other material in order to create a hard, clear, glossy surface. "Varnish" can also be used as a verb, meaning to coat something with varnish, or apply varnish to the surface.

viewing: A gathering of friends and family of a person who has died. Usually a viewing takes place at a funeral home and the coffin of the person who died is open so that people may see the person's body. You can read more about this in Chapter 4.

visitation: Similar to a viewing, except the coffin of the person who died is not necessarily open. You can read more about this in Chapter 4.

Voudon/ **Voodoo:** A mixture of customs and beliefs from the Catholic religion with customs and beliefs that African people brought with them to the island of Haiti many years ago.

wake: Another word for a gathering of friends and family of a person who has died. Wakes traditionally took place in family homes. Sometimes this is still true. The body of the person who died may or may not be present. If the body is present in the coffin, the family may have it open or closed. You can read more about this in Chapter 4.

Whanau: A Maori language word that means "extended family" and which is becoming more popular in the English language as used in New Zealand. This word is found in the resources section of this book.

How to Find Help and Support

As stated many times in this book, grief, with all of the many feelings and experiences that grief brings, is a natural and normal reaction to the death of someone dearly loved. Sometimes, people, children, teens and adults alike, feel that more help is needed to move through the process of grief. If your grief is overwhelming, if you feel that you cannot function properly, or if you simply feel that the help of someone else could be beneficial, you may want to seek out counseling or therapy.

This section is for children, teens, and their parents or caregivers. More than one person in the family may need support and help from a professional. It could be helpful for not only the child but also the parent or caregiver to examine this list, together and separately, to determine how many of these things may be true for the child as well as the parent or caregiver.

Here are some things to think about that might help you to know whether therapy or counseling might be right for you.

Check or circle any of these that are true for you:

1. ☐ My grief feels overwhelming most of the time, nearly every day.

2. ☐ I think about my grief nearly all day, nearly every day.

3. ☐ I have more times of anxiety, anger, or other painful or scary emotions than I did before grief came.

4. ☐ I have more problems concentrating since my loved one died and this has caused problems for me at home, work or school.

5. ☐   I have experienced nightmares/upsetting dreams repeatedly since my loved one's death.

6. ☐ I have experienced major changes in my eating and/or sleeping patterns.

7. ☐ I have increased health problems since my loved one died.

8. ☐ I have felt like harming myself since my loved one died.

9. ☐ I have made plans to hurt myself since my loved one died.

10. ☐ I have harmed myself since my loved one died.

11. ☐ None of these things are true for me.

I want to share something else about how I am feeling:

. . . .

. . . .

. . . .

If you or your child checked or circled any of these (other than number 11), seeking support may be very helpful. No matter what, good support is a good thing.

You may not need to see an individual therapist or counselor, and may find that group support is exactly what you need.

In the resources section you will find a listing of grief support centers that support children and their families in grief. In the grieving process, support groups can be incredibly helpful. They can help you (the parent, caregiver, or child) to know that you are not alone in your grief. You can find ways to communicate about feelings and experiences that you may have felt no one else could understand. Many groups offer ways to express feelings through expressive activities, such as drawing, painting, writing, music, movement, and play. I encourage you to seek out groups of others who have experienced a similar loss. To feel supported and understood with others who have experienced the same kind of loss is often a feeling of comfort that can be difficult to find elsewhere.

✓

If you checked or circled number 11, that doesn't mean that you are not grieving. It means that you may be experiencing something other than numbers 1–10 describe. Seeking help may still be a good thing for you. This decision should be made by you and your parent or caregiver.

If you checked or circled numbers 8, 9, or 10, you should tell someone *right away* how you are feeling. If you are a parent or caregiver, and you or your child checked any of these numbers, *seek help immediately*. If you feel that you or your child is in danger, call the emergency services number for your area. You can also find a number for crisis help in most counties and cities in the US, the UK, Canada, Australia, and New Zealand.

Most important of all, make sure that your child is safe.
Make sure that you are safe.
You can find help and you are not alone.

You can also call any of the following numbers:

In the United States:
National Hopeline Network
1 (800) SUICIDE (784–2433)

National Suicide Prevention Lifeline
1 (800) 273-TALK
For the deaf: 1 (800) 799–4889

In the UK:
Samaritans
National number: 08457 90 90 90
www.samaritans.org

Health NHS direct: 0845 46 47
www.nhsdirect.nhs.uk

Child line
Free call: 0800 1111
www.childline.org.uk

In Ireland:
Samaritans
National number: 1850 60 90 91

Child line
Free call: 1800 666 666
www.childline.org.uk

In Canada:
There are 22 help lines in 4 towns, in
5 states/countries in Canada.
Visit www.befrienders.org website to enter
your state and town to find your helpline.
www.befrienders.org/helplines/helplines.
asp?c2=Canada

In Australia:
Samaritans
24 hour service: 03 63 31 3355
www.thesamaritans.org.au

Lifeline Australia
24 hour service: 13 11 14
www.lifeline.org.au

In New Zealand:
Samaritans
24 hour service: 0800 726 666
www.thesamaritans.org.nz

Life line National:
Hotline: (64) 03 353 1136
Also visit www.suicide.org for suicide
prevention help lines and hot lines in the
US and internationally.
www.suicide.org/suicide-hotlines.html

Choosing a Therapist

Choosing a counselor or therapist is a very personal decision. The most important element in a therapeutic relationship is the relationship itself. If you trust the therapist and feel safe with him or her, this is the number one consideration. This is true for the child as well as the parent.

When choosing a therapist, you should feel comfortable with that person. You should feel comfortable with how he or she interacts with your child. Your child should also feel comfortable with that person. This section may help you in your decision making when searching for a therapist.

A common question is, "What is the difference between a counselor and a therapist?" Often, the words "therapy" and "counseling" are used to mean the same thing. They are very similar, but do have differences. In the field of mental health, counseling usually refers to a brief treatment focusing on a specific problem (like grief), and the solving of that problem. The counselor will generally offer specific suggestions and advice to help the client deal with the problem.

In practice, with a mental health professional, there is usually some overlap between counseling and psychotherapy. "Psychotherapy" is the longer term that most people simply shorten to "therapy." Often, unless a client comes in for counseling with a very specific concern (or the counselor/ therapist specializes in brief treatment), other issues more appropriately addressed through psychotherapy often come up. Psychotherapy usually involves longer treatment of many overlapping issues or problems. It involves helping the client learn more about his or her internal motives and gain insight into his or her behavior through questioning and learning about motives, needs, behavior patterns, emotions, and more. I frequently have clients come in due to a specific need or problem and, through our work together, discover other issues they would like to work on that are better dealt with through more long-term therapy. In those cases, counseling, as well as psychotherapy, are conducted with the same client.

It is important to note that while many types of counselors, including some members of clergy, such as chaplins or ministers, can provide counselling on specific issues or problems, only a trained mental health professional should conduct psychotherapy. In some cases, a student who is training to become a therapist can provide excellent therapy, but this should be done only in an approved, accredited training environment where the trainee is being supervised by a licensed professional.

The process of finding a qualified mental health professional for individual counseling and therapy is especially important when seeking a grief counselor. Currently, there are no specific requirements for being a grief counselor. Anyone can say that he or she is a grief counselor. It is true that many non-professionals, such as clergy people, or others who have a great deal of personal experience in grief and in helping others in grief, can be excellent grief counselors. However, you can narrow the process, and increase your chances of finding the right grief counselor, by starting with mental health professionals who have experience in grief.

You should not assume, however, that all mental health professionals have experience in working with grief. When deciding to work with a mental health professional, always ask about his or her experience in working with grief. Additionally, it may be difficult to find a therapist who specializes both in grief counseling and in working with people with Autism Spectrum Disorders, but this can be okay too. Whether there is a good fit depends on you, your child, and the therapist. Only you can decide whether a therapist is right for you.

Always remember that is okay to ask a therapist questions. This is true for children, teenagers, and adults. Therapy should be a partnership where you feel that you are working together with your therapist to improve your life.

Some questions you may want to ask are these:

- Do you have a license to practice therapy? (If a therapist is licensed, it means that he or she has a master's or doctoral degree level of study in the field of mental health, that he or she has completed a clinical supervised residency, and is approved by an overseeing state governing board or agency to practice his or her profession. You should be able to ask to see his or her license or the license number.)

- What is your experience in providing counseling in grief?

- Do you have experience in working with children/teenagers?

- Do you have any experience in working with children/teens/adults with ASD?

- What is your knowledge of ASD?

- How would you work with me/my child in grief?

- What can I expect as part of our therapy process?

If it is important to you and your family, you may also want to ask whether the therapist works from any particular religious or spiritual perspective.

There are several ways to find a therapist. Some people prefer to ask a trusted person for a referral. This may be a clergy person, a family member, a friend, a teacher, or a health care provider. You may want to start at your child's school with the school counselor for a referral. Grief support centers and hospices generally have lists of therapists whom they know work with grief as well as other particular issues. If you contact your local hospice or a grief support center like those listed in the resources section, they will most likely be able to give you a list of names and numbers for therapists in your area.

Additionally, the internet offers an excellent way of finding therapists. If you enter "grief therapist" into a search engine, you will find hundreds, if not thousands, of entries. If you choose to search for a therapist online, remember to search in your area.

No matter where or how you find a therapist, always remember that you should feel free to ask the questions you need to ask. If you don't feel that you have received answers that make you feel comfortable, search for another therapist. You have the right to receive good therapy from a therapist with whom you and your child are comfortable.

Grief Resources

This section includes resources for organizations online, and real world grief centers who support children and teens in grief.

International Resources

Rainbows For All Children

An international, non-profit organization, Rainbows For All Children gives children and teens the guidance to grieve and grow after loss. Rainbows goals include helping grieving youth develop and strengthen personal coping skills, learn appropriate behavior and anger management, alleviate depression, and reduce emotional pain and suffering. Schools, faith communities, agencies, and family service organizations make a commitment to partner with Rainbows to provide peer support groups in their own communities. Rainbows has programs in the US, Great Britain, Ireland, and Canada.

1-(800)–266–3206
www.rainbows.org

The MISS Foundation

The MISS Foundation is a non-profit international organization which provides immediate and on going support to grieving families, empowerment through community volunteerism opportunities, public policy and legislative education, and programs to reduce infant and toddler death through research and education. MISS provides a 24-hour, fully moderated, online support forum for kids and teens of all ages (Kids in Sympathy and Support, K.I.S.S), where they can share feelings, artwork, experiences. MISS hosts a biennial international conference, where they feature a concurrent grieving children's conference, "Kids in Sympathy and Support" camp, and teen program for children ages 5-17. MISS volunteers facilitate support groups and provide education and outreach for families in most states in the United States and internationally. Families can click on their state or consult the list of international chapters to find a support group, or call the MISS support line 24 hours a day to request a HOPE mentor to support them individually.

Toll free 1(888)455-MISS (6477)
www.missfoundation.org

The Compassionate Friends (TCF)

The Compassionate Friends mission states that they provide comfort, hope, and support to every family experiencing the death of a son or daughter, a brother or sister, or a grandchild, and helps others better assist the grieving family. They have chapter groups and support meetings all over the world and offer support to parents,

siblings, and grandparents of children who have died. TCF also supports international, national and regional conferences for members and professionals. TCF supports organizations in the US, the UK, Australia, Belgium, Canada, France, Germany, Philippines, and South Africa.
United States TCF
Call toll-free: 1-(877) 969-0010
www.compassionatefriends. org/home.aspx

Twinless Twins Support Group International

The Twinless Twins Support Group International (TTSGI) provides support for twins and other multiples of any age who are grieving the death or estrangement of their twin or multiple(s). They are a nonprofit international organization founded by an identical twin who found help for himself by reaching out to other twinless twins. They provide support to twins through regional activities, national conferences and educational support.
United States, Canada, United Kingdom and Australia
www.twinlesstwins.org

The Dougy Center

The Dougy Center provides training internationally for professionals and organizations in how to set up and operate a grief support facility for children and their families, based on their highly successful initial model in Portland, Oregon. (See section on United States resources for Dougy Center contact information.)

Child and Adolescent Mental Health Services (CAMHS)

Child and Adolescent Mental Health Services is a part of the United Kingdom's National Health Service and Australia's Department of Health. CAMHS offers help for children and young people experiencing emotional, behavioural, and mental health difficulties. CAMHS provides consultation, support, and full psychological and psychiatric services. The UK national website has a Teen Zone where teens can share art, poetry and film to express their feelings.

United Kingdom

You can phone National Health Services (NHS) direct to inquire about your local CAMHS at **0845 4647**

Australia

South Australia's division of CAMHS at Women's and Children's Hospital provides Western, Eastern, Northern and Country Community Services. They also offer the Aboriginal Mental Health Partnership, which is involved in developing and providing services to Aboriginal children, young people, and families who are at risk of mental health difficulties.
618 8161 7198
www.wch.sa.gov.au/services/az/ divisions/mentalhealth/index.html

National Resources

This section includes names and contact information for overall national support, as well as grief support centers that specifically provide support for children, teens, and their families in grief.

The centers listed here are dedicated to providing grief support for children, teens, and their families. Some provide peer support groups, arts and expressive therapies groups, referrals for individual therapy and counseling, in-school groups, and other kinds of family support. Please consult the website, and email or call the center for specific information about services provided by each center.

Additionally, many local hospices offer grief support groups for adults and children, as well as referrals for counseling and other support. Many hospices offer extensive supports for grieving children. These services are often offered to the general public, and not just patients and families who have received care from the hospice. You are encouraged to call your local hospices for information on groups and support for children.

United States of America

The National Alliance for Grieving Children

The National Alliance for Grieving Children is a national service that provides an extensive list of grief support centers for children nationwide. They also offer support and resources for professionals, schools, and families, as well as conferences, trainings, and information on grief research.
(866) 432-1542
http://childrengrieve.org

Sesame Street Workshop—**"When Families Grieve"**
Sesame Street Workshop created outreach materials to support children grieving the death of a loved one. They have partnered with hospices, grief support and children's grief centers all over the United States to distribute "When Families Grieve," a grief kit for families who have experienced the death of a loved one. There is a version of the outreach kit created especially for military families. All accompanying guidebooks are in English and in Spanish. Each kit contains a Sesame Street DVD, a guidebook for parents and caregivers, and a story. Please visit the website for further information or to view their videos online.
www.sesameworkshop.org/grief

STATE BY STATE LISTING OF GRIEF CENTERS OFFERING SUPPORT FOR CHILDREN AND TEENS:

ALABAMA
Amelia Center
1513 4th Avenue South
Birmingham, AL 35233
(205)-251-3430
www.ameliacenter.org

The Healing Place
2409 Wildwood Street, POB 2765
Muscle Shoals, AL 35662
(256)-3837133
www.thehealingplaceinfo.org

ALASKA
Forget Me Not Grief Program
500 West International Airport Road,
Suite C
Anchorage AK 99518
(907)-561-5322
**www.hospiceofanchorage.
org/ForgetMeNot.htm**

ARIZONA
**The New Song Center for Grieving
Children**
6947 East McDonald Drive
Scottsdale AZ 85253
(480)-951-8985
www.hov.org/new_song_center.aspx

**Tu Nidito ("your little nest")
Children and Family Services**
39252 North Mountain Avenue
Tucson, AZ 85719
(530)-322-9155
www.tunidito.org

Stepping Stones of Hope
(602)-264-7520
www.steppingstonesofhope.org

ARKANSAS
Center for Good Mourning
Arkansas Children's Hospital
1 Children's Way
Little Rock AR 72202
(501)-364-1100
**www.archildrens.org/Services/
Center-for-Good-Mourning.aspx**

Kaleidoscope Kids
Arkansas Children's Hospital East Campus
1621 W. 10th St. Little Rock, AR 72202
(501)-978-5437
http://kaleidoscopekids.org

CALIFORNIA
Josie's Place
3288 21st Street, Suite 139
San Francisco CA 94110
(415)-513-6343
http://josiesplace.org

Kara Grief
457 Kingsley Avenue
Palo Alto CA 94301
(650)-321-5272
www.kara-grief.org

Mourning Star
42–600 Cook Street, Suite 202
Palm Desert CA 92211
Palm Desert location (760)-836-0360
Victorville location (760)-948-7249
Riverside location (951)-413-1387
www.mourningstar.org

Camp Hope
5535 Arroyo Road
Livermore, CA 94550
No phone number available. Contact
through email via Camp Hope's website.
http://camphopeca.com

Gary's Place for Kids
23332 Mill Creek Drive, Suite 230
Laguna Hills CA 92653
(949)-348-0548
www.gpfk.org

Our House Grief Support Center
1663 Sawtelle Blvd., Suite 300,
Los Angeles CA 90025
(818)-222-3344
www.ourhouse-grief.org

**New Hope Grief Support
Community**
**(562)-429-0075 or toll-
free (888)-490-HOPE**
www.newhopegrief.org

Teen Age Grief Inc.
(818)-858-3401 http://
teenagegrief.org

**WillMar Family Grief and Healing
Center**
(707)-935-1946
www.willmarcenter.org

COLORADO
Judi's House
1741 Gaylord Street
Denver CO 80206
(720)-941-0331
www.judishouse.org

The Light House
2379 South High Street
Denver CO 80210
(303)-722-2319
http://childgrief.org/childgrief.htm

CONNECTICUT
The Center for Hope
590 Post Road
Darien, CT 06820
(203)-869-4848
www.centerforhope.org

**The Cove Center for Grieving
Children**
250 Pomeroy Avenue, Suite 107
Meriden, CT 06450
(203)-634-0500
www.covect.org

Mary's Place
6 Poquonick Avenue
Windsor, CT 06095
(860)-688-9621
http://marysplacect.org

Safe Place to Grieve Foundation
109 Main Street
Wethersfield, CT 06109
(860)-563-5677
http://safeplacetogrievefoundation.
org

DELAWARE
**Supporting Kidds—a Center
for Grieving Children and their
Families**
1213 Old Lancaster Pike
Hockessin DE 19707
(302)-235-5544
www.supportingkidds.org

DISTRICT OF COLUMBIA/
WASHINGTON D.C.
Wendt Center for Healing and Loss
4201 Connecticut Avenue NW
Washington D.C. 20008
(202)-624-0010
www.wendtcenter.org

FLORIDA
**Tomorrow's Rainbow—Equine
Assisted Grief Support for Children**
4341 NW 39th Avenue
Coconut Creek, FL 33073
(954)-978-2390
www.tomorrowsrainbow.org

Children's Bereavement Center
7600 S. Red Road, Suite 307
Miami, FL 33143
(305)-668-4902
www.childbereavement.org

New Hope for Kids
205 East SR 436
Fern Park, FL 32730
(407)-331-3059
http://newhopeforkids.org

Sun Coast Kid's Place
17030 Lakeshore Road
Lutz, FL 33558
(813)-990-0216
www.suncoastkidsplace.org

Kathy's Place 4 Hope
730 South Sterling Avenue
Tampa FL 33609
(813)875-0728
http://aplace4hope.org

GEORGIA

Kate's Club, Inc.
1330 West Peachtree Street NW
Suite 520
Atlanta, GA 30309
(404) 347-7619
www.katesclub.org

Project KARMA, Inc.
PO Box 89311
Atlanta, GA 30312
(404) 207-9980
www.project-karma.org

**Camp MAGIK—Mainly About Grief
In Kids**
3377 Ridgewood Road, NW
Atlanta, GA 30327
www.campmagik.org

Hope for Grieving Children
710 Mimosa Boulevard
Roswell, GA 30075
(770) 915-2537
http://rfbc.org

The House Next Door
348 Mt. Vernon Hwy. NE
Atlanta, GA 30328
(404) 256-9797
http://thelink.org

HAWAII

**Kids Hurt Too—Outreach for
Grieving Youth Alliance**
245 North Kukui Street, Suite 203
Honolulu, HI 96817
(808) 545-5683
www.kidshurttoo.org

IDAHO

**Willow Center for Grieving
Children**
PO Box 1361
Lewiston, Idaho 83501

(509) 780-1156
www.willow-center.org

**The Touchstone Center for Grieving
Children and Adolescents**
3800 Shady Glen
Boise, ID 83712
(208) 377-3216
http://touchstonecenter.org

ILLINOIS

Barr-Harris Children's Grief Center
122 S. Michigan Avenue, Suite 1300
Chicago, IL 60603
312-922-7474 ext 310
www.barrharris.org

Buddy's Place of Pillars
1023 Burlington Avenue
Western Springs, IL 60558
(708) 995-3750
www.pillarscommunity.org

Willow House
302 Saunders Road, Suite 200
Riverwoods, IL 60015
(847) 236-9300
http://willowhouse.org

**Center for Grief Recovery: Institute
for Creativity**
1263 W. Loyola, Suite 100
Chicago, IL 60626
(773) 274-4600
www.griefcounselor.org

INDIANA

**Brooke's Place for Grieving Young
People**
50 E. 91st Street, Suite 103
Indianapolis, IN 46240
(317) 705-9650
www.brookesplace.org

Ryan's Place
PO Box 73
Goshen, IN 46527
(574) 535-1000
www.ryans-place.org

Erin's House for Grieving Children
Parkwest Center and Administration
3811 Illinois Road, Suite 205
Fort Wayne, IN 46804
(260) 423-2466
http://erinshouse.org

IOWA
Amanda the Panda
1000 73rd Street Suite 12
Windsor Heights, IA 50324
(515) 223-4847
www.amandathepanda.org

Rick's House of Hope for Grieving and Traumatized Children
1227 East Rusholme Street
Davenport, IA 52803
(563) 324-9580
http://genesishealth.com

KANSAS
Kidzcope
9415 East Harry, Suite 501
Wichita, KS 67207
(316) 263-3335
www.kidzcope.org

The Guidance Center
500 Limit Street
Leavenworth, KS 66048
(913) 682-5118
www.guidance-center.org

Solace House
8012 State Line Road, Suite 202
Prairie Village, KS 66208
(913) 341-0318
www.solacehouse.org

KENTUCKY
STARS: Grief Support for Kids
483 South Loop Drive
Edgewood, KY 41017
(859) 292-0244
Website unavailable.

The Grief Connection—Gilda's Club Louisville
633 Baxter Avenue
Louisville. KY 40204-1157
(502) 583-0075
www.gildasclublouisville.org

LOUISIANA
Healing House: Hope for Grieving Children
PO Box 3861
Lafayette, LA 70502
(337) 234-0443
www.healing-house.org

Seasons Grief and Loss Center
654 Brockenbraugh Court
Metairie, LA 70005
(504) 834-5957
www.seasonsgriefcenter.org

A Place That Warms the Heart
3410 Shadow Wood Drive
Haughton, LA 71037
(318) 671-7747
http://placethatwarmstheheart.fws1.com

Project SKY/Grief Recovery Center
4919 Jamestown Avenue, Suite 102
Baton Rouge, LA 70808
(225) 924-6621
No website available.

MAINE
The Center for Grieving Children
555 Forest Avenue
Portland, ME 04101
(207) 775-5216
http://cgcmaine.org

Healing Circle for Grieving Children
PO Box 688
Caribou, ME 04736
(207) 498-2578
No website available.

A Program for Grieving Children and Teens
PO Box 819
Lewiston, ME 04243
(207) 777-7740
No website available.

Camp Ray of Hope—Hospice Volunteers of Waterville Area
304 Main Street, PO Box 200
Waterville, ME 04901
(207) 873-3615
www.hvwa.org/camp-ray-of-hope.shtml

MARYLAND
Roberta's House
1900 N. Broadway
Baltimore, MD 21213
(410) 235-6633
www.robertashouse.org

Teens Learning to Grieve[AQ]
2914 East Joppa Road, Suite 204
Baltimore, MD 21234
(410) 668-0324
childrengrieve.org/programs-maryland

MASSACHUSETTS
The Children's Room: Center for Grieving Children and Teens, Inc.
1210 Massachusetts Avenue
Arlington, MA 02476
(781) 641-4741
http://childrensroom.org

Jeff's Place and Manitou Experience
PO Box 5072
Wayland, MA 01778
(508) 276-3225
www.manitouexperience.org

Circle of Tapawingo
2251 Commonwealth Ave
Auburndale, MA 02466
(781) 820-3388
www.circleoftapawingo.org

Rick's Place, Inc.
35 Post Office Park, Suite 3514
Wilbraham, MA 01095
(413) 348-3120
www.ricksplacema.org

Children's Friend
20 Cedar Street
Worcester, MA 01609
(508) 753-5425
http://childrensfriend.org

MICHIGAN
Ele's Place (Lansing location)
1145 W. Oakland Avenue
Lansing, MI 48915
(517) 482-1315
www.elesplace.org

Ele's Place (Ann Arbor location)
355 S. Zeeb Road, Suite E
Ann Arbor, MI 48103
(734) 929-6640
www.elesplace.org

Gilda's Club Grand Rapids
1806 Bridge Street NW
Grand Rapids, MI 49504
(616) 453-8300
www.gildasclubgr.org

SandCastles Grief Support Program
1 Ford Place, 4A
Detroit, MI 48202
(313) 874-6881
Locations in Detroit, Clinton Township, Livonia, St. Clair Shores, Southfield, Down River/South Gate, Rochester, West Bloomfield, and Ortonville, MI
http://aboutsandcastles.org/index.html

CAMP Live, Laugh, Love
Children's Bereavement Network
PO Box 181
Gaylord, MI 49734
(800) 861-8418
www.camplivelaughlove.org

Yatooma's Foundation For the Kids
219 Elm Street
Birmingham, MI 48009-6306
(888) 987-5437
http://forthekidsfoundation.org

New Hope Center for Grief Support
113 E. Dunlap
Northville, MI 48167
(248) 348-0115
http://newhopecenter.net

MINNESOTA
Children's Grief Connection
72351 Pine River Road
Willow River, MN 55795
(877) 226-7632
www.childrensgriefconnection.com

**Youth Grief Services/Spiritual
Health Services**
201 East Nicollet Boulevard
Burnsville, MN 55337
(952) 892-2111
www.youthgriefservices.org

MISSISSIPPI
The McClean Fletcher Center
12 Northtown Drive
Jackson, MS 39211
(601) 206-5525
www.mccleanfletcher.org

MISSOURI
**Annie's Hope—The Bereavement
Center for Kids**
1333 W. Lockwood, Suite 104
St. Louis, MO 63122
(314) 965-5015
http://annieshope.org

Lost and Found Grief Center
1006 N. Cedarbrook Avenue
Springfield, MO 65802
(417) 865-9998
http://lostandfoundozarks.com

MONTANA
Tamarack Grief Resource Center
516 South Orange Street
Missoula, MT 59801
(406) 541-8472
www.tamarackgriefresourcecenter.org

NEBRASKA
Mourning Hope Grief Center
4919 Baldwin Avenue
Lincoln, NE 68504
(402) 488-8989
www.mourninghope.org

Ted E. Bear Hollow
347 North 76th Street
Omaha, NE 68114–3627
(402) 502-2773
www.tedebearhollow.org

Charlie Brown's Kids—Good Grief
PO Box 67106
Lincoln, NE 68506
(402) 483-1845
http://charliebrownskids.org

NEVADA
The Solace Tree
PO Box 2944
Reno, NV 89505
(775) 324-7723
www.solacetree.org

Adam's Place
5017 Alta Drive
Las Vegas, NV 89107
(702) 481-1996
http://adamsplaceforgrief.org

NEW HAMPSHIRE
Bridges for Children and Teens
10 Hampton Road
Exeter, NH 03833
(603) 778-7391
http://seacoasthospice.org

Pete's Place
30 St.Thomas Street, Suite 240
Dover, NH 03820
(603) 740-2689
No website available.

Good Mourning Children
54 Blackberry Lane
Keene, NH 03431-2120
(603) 352-7799
No website available.

NEW JERSEY
The Alcove Center for Grieving Children and Families
950 Tilton Road, Suite 108
Northfield, NJ 08225
(609) 484-1133
www.thealcove.org

Comfort Zone Camp North
80 Park Street
Montclair, NJ 07042
(973) 364-1717
http://comfortzonecamp.org

Common Ground Grief Center
67 Taylor Avenue
Manasquan, NJ 08736
Phone: 732-606-7477
www.commongroundgriefcenter.org

Good Grief, Inc.
38 Elm Street
Morristown, NJ 07960
(908) 522-1999
www.good-grief.org

Imagine, a Center for Coping with Loss
1 East Broad Street
Westfield, NJ 07090
(908) 264-3100
www.imaginenj.org

Hearts and Crafts Grief Counseling
60 E. Main Street
Ramsey, NJ 07446
(201) 818-9399
www.heartsandcraftscounseling.org

NEW MEXICO
Children's Grief Center of New Mexico
3020 Morris NE
Albuquerque, NM 87111
(505) 323-0478
http://childrensgrief.org

Gerard's House
PO Box 28693
Santa Fe, NM 87592
(505) 424-1800
http://gerardshouse.org

Golden Willow Retreat
PO Box 569
Arroyo Hondo, NM 87513
(505) 776-2024
http://goldenwillowretreat.org

NEW YORK
The Bereavement Center of Westchester Tree House
69 Main Street
Tuckahoe, NY 10707
(914) 961-2818 ext 317
http://thebereavementcenter.org

Camp Good Grief of Staten Island Inc.
1076 Forest Avenue
Staten Island, NY 10310
(518) 506-5999
http://campgoodgriefsi.org

COPE
PO Box 1251
Melville, NY 11747
(516) 484-4993
www.copefoundation.org

Friends of Karen, Inc.
118 Titicus Road, PO Box 190
Purdy's, NY 10578
(800) 637-2774
http://friendsofkaren.org

A Caring Hand, the Billy Esposito Foundation and Bereavement Center
305 Seventh Avenue, 16th floor
New York, NY 10001
(212) 561-0622
http://acaringhand.org

The Sanctuary
PO Box 795
Larchmont, NY 10538
(914) 834-4906
http://thesanctuaryforgrief.org

NORTH CAROLINA
KinderMourn
1320 Harding Place
Charlotte, NC 28204
(704) 376-2580
http://Kindermourn.org

National Students of AMF Support Network
3344 Hillsborough St.
Raleigh, NC 27607
(919) 803-6728
www.studentsofamf.org

Kids Path of Hospice and Palliative Care of Greensboro
Greensboro, NC 27405
(336) 544-5437
http://kidspath.com

NORTH DAKOTA
Contact your local hospice for information about grief support for children and families.

OHIO
Bobby's Books
555 Metro Place North, Suite 650
Dublin, OH 43017
(614) 763-0036
www.bobbysbooks.org

Companions on a Journey Grief Support, Inc.
5475 Creek Bend Drive
West Chester, OH 45069
(513) 870-9108
www.companionsonajourney.org

Cornerstone of Hope
5905 Brecksville Road
Independence, OH 44131
(216) 524-3787
www.cornerstoneofhope.org

Fernside for Grieving Children and Families
4380 Malsbary Road
Cincinnati, OH 45242
(513) 745-0111
www.fernside.org

Joel's Place for Children
PO Box 180
Avon, OH 44011
(440) 248-4412
www.joelsplaceforchildren.org

Oak Tree Corner, Inc.
2312 Far Hills Box 108
Dayton, OH 45419
(937) 285-0199
http://oaktreecorner.com

The Gathering Place
23300 Commerce Pk.
Beachwood, OH 44122
(216) 595-9546
http://touchedbycancer.org

The Treehouse
2421 Auburn Avenue
Cincinnati, OH 45219
(513) 731-3346
http://cancerfamilycare.org

OKLAHOMA
Calm Waters Center for Children and Families
4334 NW Expressway, Suite 101
Oklahoma City, OK 73116
(405) 841-4800
Website unavailable.

The Kids' Place
601 S. Bryant Avenue
Edmond, OK 73034
(405) 844-5437
www.edmondkids.org

OREGON
The Dougy Center
PO Box 86852
Portland, OR 97286
(503) 775-5683
http://dougy.org

My Friend's House, Inc.
2075 NE Wyatt Court
Bend, OR 97701
(541) 382-5882
www.partnersbend.org/Grief-and-Loss/Children%27s-Grief-Support

Winterspring
PO Box 8169
Medford, OR 97501
(541) 772-2527
http://winterspring.org

PENNSYLVANIA
Camp Koala
201 N. Hanover St.
Carlisle, PA 17013
(717) 258-1122
www.campkoala.org

The Center for Grieving Children, Teens and Families
1139 East Luzerne Street
Philadelphia, PA 19124
(215) 744-4025
www.grievingchildren.org

Drew Michael Taylor Foundation-Drew's Hope
402 Richwalter Avenue
Shippensburg, PA 17257
(717) 532-8922
www.drewmichaeltaylor.org

Highmark Caring Place—a Center for Grieving Children, Adolescents and Their Families
Pittsburg location
620 Stanwix Street
Pittsburgh, PA 15222
(888) 224-4673
www.highmarkcaringplace.com

Highmark Caring Place—a Center for Grieving Children, Adolescents and Their Families
Erie location
Bayview Office Park, Building 2
510 Cranberry Street
Erie, PA 16507
(866) 212-4673
www.highmarkcaringplace.com

Highmark Caring Place—a Center for Grieving Children, Adolescents and Their Families
Lemoyne location
3 Walnut Street, Suite 200
Lemoyne, PA 17043
(866) 613-4673
www.highmarkcaringplace.com

Highmark Caring Place—a Center for Grieving Children, Adolescents and Their Families
Warrendale location
200 Warrendale Village Drive
Warrendale, PA 15222
(888) 743-4073
www.highmarkcaringplace.com

Olivia's House
830 S George Street
York, PA 17403
(717) 699-1133
http://oliviashouse.org

PATHways Center for Grief and Loss
4025 Old Harrisburg Pike
Mt. Joy, PA 17552
(717) 391-2413
www.pathwaysthroughgrief.org

Peter's Place
150 Radnor–Chester Road, Suite F130
Radnor, PA 19087
(610) 687-5150
http://petersplaceonline.org

Precious Gems Supportive Services
231 South Easton Road
Glenside, PA 19038
(888) 526-6958
http://preciousgems.org

TIDES—Support Program for Grieving Children
PO Box 1251
State College, PA 16804
(814) 692-2233
http://tidesprogram.org

Mommy's Light Lives On
PO Box 494
Lionville, PA 19353
(610) 458-1690
http://mommyslight.org

Daddy's Spirit Moves Me Forward
PO Box 80022
Valley Forge, PA 19484
(610) 710-1477
http://DaddysSpirit.org

RHODE ISLAND
Friends Way
765 West Shore Road
Warwick RI 02889
(401) 921-0980
www.friendsway.org

SOUTH CAROLINA
Jamie's Tree House
1304 Springdale Drive
Clinton, SC 29325
(864) 833-6287
http://hospiceoflaurenscounty.com

Katherine's Camp
PO Box 151
Drayton, SC 29333
(864) 641-8227
www.facebook.com/pages/
Katherines-Camp/154999527859006

TENNESSEE
Contact your local hospice for information about grief support for children and families.

TEXAS
Bo's Place
10050 Buffalo Speedway
Houston, TX 77054
(713) 942-8339
http://bosplace.org

Children's Bereavement Center of South Texas
205 W. Olmos
San Antonio, TX 78212
(210) 736-4847
www.cbcst.org

Children's Grief Center of El Paso
11625 Pellicano, Suite B
El Paso, TX 79936
(915) 532-6004
http://cgcelpaso.org

For the Love of Christi
2306 Hancock Drive
Austin, TX 78756
(512) 467-2600
http://fortheloveofchristi.org

GriefWorks
6320 LBJ Freeway, Suite 126
Dallas, TX 75240
(800) 375-2229
www.grief-works.org

The Hope and Healing Place
1721 S. Tyler
Amarillo, TX 79102
(806) 371-8998
http://hopeandhealingplace.org

Journey of Hope Grief Support Center
3900 West 15th Street, Suite 306
Plano, TX 75075
(972) 964-1600
http://johgriefsupport.org

Rays of Hope Children's Grief Centre
900 West Wall Street
Midland, TX 79701
(432) 684-KIDS (5437)
http://raysofhopemidland.org

The WARM Place
809 Lipscomb Street
Fort Worth, TX 76104-3121
(817) 870-2272
http://thewarmplace.org

El Tesoro de la Vida Grief Camp— Camp Fire USA First Texas Council
2700 Meacham Blvd.
Fort Worth, TX 76137-4699
(817) 831-2111
www.CampElTesoro.org

Project Joy and Hope for Texas
PO Box 5111
Pasadena, TX 77508
(866) JOY-HOPE
http://joyandhope.org

My Healing Place
405 W. 22nd Street
Austin, TX 78705
(512) 472-7878
http://myhealingplace.org

UTAH
The Sharing Place
1695 East 3300 South
Salt Lake City, UT 84106
(801) 466-6730
www.thesharingplace.org

The Family Summit Foundation-A Center For Grieving Children
560 39th Street
Ogden, UT 84403
(801) 476-1127
http://familysummit.com

VIRGINIA
Full Circle Grief Center— Richmond's Family Grief Center
10611 Patterson Avenue, Building 201
Richmond, VA 23238
(804) 912-2947
www.fullcirclegriefcenter.org

Comfort Zone Camp
4906 Cutshaw Avenue, 2nd floor
Richmond, VA 23230
(804) 377-3430
www.comfortzonecamp.org

Jewish Family Services—Dozoretz Center for Family Healing
260 Grayson Road
Virginia Beach, VA 23462
(757) 459-4640
www.jfshamptonroads.org

Kids' Haven: A Center for Grieving Children
325 12th Street
Lynchburg, VA 24504
(434) 845-4072
www.kidshavenlynchburg.org

VERMONT
Center for Creative Healing
114 Westminster Road
Putney, VT 05346
(802) 387-2550
www.center4creativehealing.com

WASHINGTON
Camp Erin
The Moyer Foundation
2426 32nd Avenue West
Seattle, WA 98199
(206) 298-1217
www.moyerfoundation.org

The Healing Center
640901/2 Roosevelt Way NE
Seattle, WA 98115
(206) 523-1206
http://healingcenterseattle.org

BRIDGES: A Center for Grieving Children
310 North K Street
Tacoma, WA 98403
(253) 272-8266
www.multicare.org/marybridge/

Rise N' Shine
417 23rd Avenue South
Seattle, WA 98144
(206) 628-8949
http://risenshine.org

Journey Program
4800 Sandpoint Way NE
Seattle, WA 98105-9907
(866) 987-2000
http://seattlechildrens.org

Camp Amanda
Walla Walla Community Hospice
1067 Isaacs Avenue
Walla Walla, WA 99362
(509) 525-5561
http://wwhospice.org/children.htm

WISCONSIN
MargaretAnn's Place
912 N Hawley Road
Milwaukee, WI 53213
(414) 732-2663
www.margaretannsplace.org

Faith's Lodge
6942 Country Road C
Danbury WI 54830
(715) 866-8200
www.faithslodge.org

Camp HOPE
301 Florence Drive
Stevens Point, WI 54482
(715) 341-0076
http://camphopeforkids.org

Kyle's Korner
7106 W. North Avenue
Wauwatosa, WI 53213
(414) 777-1585
http://kyleskorner.org

Mourning Cloak
120 W. Dodge St.
Port Washington, WI 53074
(414) 704-7640
www.mourningcloak.org

United Kingdom

Winston's Wish
United Kingdom National Helpline
(UK only) 08452 03 04 05
For general information in the
UK phone **01242 515157.**
www.winstonswish.org.uk

**STARS Children's Bereavement
Service**
c/o CPDC
Foster Road
Trumpington, Cambridge
CB2 9NL
In the UK phone **01223
863511** or **07827 74349.**
www.talktostars.org.uk

**The Childhood Bereavement
Network (CBN)**
This organization provides support for
those working with grieving children,
young people, and their families across the
UK.
0207 843 6309
**www.childhoodbereavementnetwork.
org.uk**

Canada

Good Grief Resource Centre
936 Lorne Avenue, London Ontario
N5W 3L1
(519) 697-4541
www.patchforkids.ca

Camp Kerry
Camp Kerry Society
#200-8081 Lougheed Highwsy
Burnaby, British Columbia, Canada
V5A 1W9
(604) 608-9859
http://campkerry.org

Circle of Life
#216, 9804 100 Ave.
Grande Prairie, Alberta
T8V 0T8
(780) 539-5432
www.circleoflifegp.com/index.html

Grieving Children Lighthouse
82 Wilson Street
Oakville, Ontario
L6K 3G5
905-337-2333
www.grievingchildrenlighthouse.org

**Seasons Centre for Grieving
Children**
38 McDonald Street,
Barrie, Ontario
L4M 1P1
705-721-KIDS (5437)
www.grievingchildren.com

Australia

**Australian Centre for Grief and
Bereavement—Kids Grieve Too**
McCulloch House, Monash Medical Centre
246 Clayton Road, Clayton,
Victoria 3168 Australia
phone +61 3 9265 2100
Free call Australia-wide **1800 642 066**
www.grief.org.au

Australian Kids Help
Free call phone line available 24 hours a
day, seven days a week, for children and
young people aged 5 to 25.
Australia-wide free call at **1800 551 800**
Kids Helpline Administration
GPO Box 2469
Brisbane Queensland 4001
Administration phone: **07 3369 1588**
(not a counseling service line)
www.kidshelp.com.au

Australia National SIDS and Kids—Healing Families
Locations in ACT Region, Hunter, New South Wales, Northern Territory, Queensland, South Australia, Tasmania, Victoria, Western Australia.

SIDS and Kids Australia
Suite 1, 98 Morang Road
Hawthorn Victoria 3122
Phone: **+61 3 9819 4595**
www.sidsandkids.org

Bereavement Care Centre
PO Box 835, Wyong, New South Wales, 2259

Phone **1300 654 556**
www.bereavementcare.com.au/index.htm

A Friend's Place—The National Centre for Childhood Grief
PO Box 327
Epping, New South Wales 1710
Phone **1300 654 556**
www.childhoodgrief.org.au

New Zealand

Skylight
PO Box 7309, Newtown,
Wellington 6242
0800 299 100 or **04 939 6767**
www.skylight.org.nz

Autism Resources

For more information and support for Autism Spectrum Disorder (ASD)

The Autism Society
The Autism Society, founded in 1965, is the leading grass-roots autism organization in the United States. They state that they exist to help improve the lives of all people affected by autism. There are chapters nationwide.
www.autism-society.org

Autism Speaks
The United States' largest science-based autism advocacy group, Autism Speaks was founded in 2005 and is dedicated to funding research into autism. Autism Speaks lists hundreds of autism support organizations throughout the world on their "what is autism" page.
www.autismspeaks.org

Autism Spectrum Australia (Aspect)
Aspect is the largest not-for-profit autism service provider in Australia. They strive to build confidence and capacity in people with ASD, their families, and communities by providing information, education, and other services. Their website has much information on all aspects of ASD and they offer direct services in the Australian Capital Territory (ACT), New South Wales (NSW) and Victoria.
www.autismspectrum.org.au

Autism Canada
Autism Canada is a registered charitable organization that is dedicated to improving the lives of Canadians affected by autism. They provide information on research, treatments, resources, and how the lives of those on the spectrum are impacted by autism.
www.autismcanada.org

Autism New Zealand Inc.

Autism New Zealand Inc. provides support, training, advocacy, resources and information on autism spectrum disorders for the people of New Zealand. Their members include children, young adults and adults on the autism spectrum; their family, **whanau**, caregivers, as well as professionals who work in the field of autism. They provide advocacy, information, support, training (including for early intervention programs), and more for families and professionals.

Do2Learn

The Do2learn website provides thousands of pages of social skills and behavioral regulation activities and guidance, learning songs and games, communication cards, academic material, and transition guides for employment and life skills. They provide instruction on how to make and use visual schedules, cues and other strategies, how to adapt environments for children with ASD, how to write and implement behavior support plans and more. Designed for teachers, these tools can also be used in the home environment.
www.do2learn.com

The Gray Center

The Gray Center, founded by Carol Gray, educator and expert in the field of social communication for people with autism, is dedicated to providing help and support for people with autism, to cultivating their strengths and promoting global understanding. The website carries a wealth of information and provides help with communication, parenting, building social connections, and more. Information about Social Stories™ is available here.
www.thegraycenter.org/social-stories

The National Autistic Society

The leading charity in the United Kingdom for people on the autism spectrum, the National Autistic Society strives for a world where all people living with autism get to live the life they choose. They work toward increasing understanding of autism and helping those on the spectrum get the help they need. They have sites in England, Northern Ireland, Scotland, and Wales.
www.autism.org.uk

TEACCH (Treatment and Education of Autistic and Communication Handicapped Children/Adults)

The University of North Carolina TEACCH Autism Program, founded in 1972, creates and cultivates the development of exemplary community-based services, training programs, and research to enhance the quality of life for individuals with ASD and their families. The TEACCH approach centers on the individual with ASD and his or her strengths, needs, skills, and interests. They strive to promote understanding of a "culture of autism," meaning that people with ASD have characteristics that are different, not inferior, to those of others who do not have ASD. The website is an excellent source of resources and information for those interested in promoting the individuality of each person on the autism spectrum.
www.teacch.com

Books

There are many books on grief and bereavement, and also on grief and bereavement for children and teenagers. As this is primarily a book for children and teens with Autism Spectrum Disorder, I will list books that I feel might be particularly helpful for this population and their families.

Books for Children and Teens

Carney, Karen (2001) *What is Cancer, Anyway? Explaining Cancer to Children of All Ages.* **Wethersfield, CT: Dragonfly Publishing.**
This is a coloring book for children that presents technical information about cancer in a direct but comforting way.

Goldman, Linda (2006) *Children Also Grieve: Talking About Death and Healing.* **London: Jessica Kingsley Publishers.**
This is a fully illustrated interactive storybook that helps young children come to terms with the death of a significant loved one. The story tells the experiences of Henry, the family dog, after his grandfather has died. The book contains a memory book/journaling section that uses prompts to help guide children through different aspects of the grief process.

Grollman, Earl, Johnson, Joy and Donner, Brad (2006) *A Complete Book About Death for Kids.* **(Omaha, NE): Centering Corporation.**
A guide for children by bereavement experts that includes a section about the different feelings that may be experienced in grief, another section about various rituals and funeral practices and includes photographs of what a child may actually see.

Heegard, Marge (1991) *When Something Terrible Happens: Children can Learn to Cope with Grief.* **Minneapolis, MN: Woodland Press.**
The cover of the book states that the book is to be illustrated by children. It is a drawing and activities book for young children learning to manage the feelings and changes in life after a tragic event has occurred. The format encourages and allows the child to use both art and language.

Johnston, Tony and Winter, Jeanette (1997) *Day of the Dead.* **San Diego, CA: Harcourt Brace and Co.**
A colorful book, beautifully illustrated by Jeanette Winter, that follows a Mexican family from sunrise on *El Dia De Los Muertos* to the night when they honor their loved ones. The end of the book also contains factual information about the holiday. This lovely book is a great addition to any Day of the Dead enthusiast's collection.

Krementz, Jill (1981) *How it Feels When a Parent Dies.* **New York, NY: Knopf.**
Eighteen children aged 7 to 17 who have experienced grief due to the death of a parent share their personal stories. Photographs of the child with his or her surviving parent are included.

Stickney, Doris (1997) *Waterbugs and Dragonflies: Explaining Death to Young Children.* **Cleveland, OH: Pilgrim Press.**

This is a classic, short, read-along book that uses the transformation of the dragonfly to explain death to children. It compares the dragonfly's metamorphosis to a loved one's spiritual transformation after death of the physical body. I love this book for all ages. This book was given to me after my son died. I found it beautiful and I read it to all participants, of all ages, who come to my grief support groups.

Books for Parents and Children

Atwood, Tony (2004) *Exploring Feelings: Cognitive Behaviour Therapy to Manage Anxiety.* **Arlington, TX: Future Horizons, Inc.**

Atwood, Tony (2004) *Exploring Feelings: Cognitive Behaviour Therapy to Manage Anger.* **Arlington, TX: Future Horizons, Inc.**

These books are behavior programs in workbook style to be used by children experiencing anxiety or anger. Dr. Attwood's programs help the child with Asperger's explore and manage those difficult emotions, both of which are often increased during times of grieving. The feelings, and managing of those feelings, are presented from a scientific perspective with a metaphor of the child as a scientist or astronaut exploring a new planet. The workbooks are highly structured and are designed for individual responses rather than for groups.

Faherty, Catherine (2008) *Understanding Death and Illness and What They Teach About Life: An Interactive Guide for Individuals with Autism or Asperger's and Their Loved Ones.* **Arlington, TX: Future Horizons, Inc.**

This excellent book addresses illness, injury, death, dying, grief and other difficult topics in a style that is easily understood by all age groups of people on and off the autism spectrum. The book contains a workbook style "communication forms" which encourage the reader to share his or her personal observations, thoughts, feelings and what is true or not true for them. The range of topics covered is immense. Highly recommended for any family of a person on the autism spectrum who is dealing with the terminal illness or death of a loved one, including pets.

Gray, Carol (2010) *The New Social Story™ Book. Revised and Expanded 10th Anniversary Edition: Over 150 Social Stories that Teach Everyday Social Skills to Children with Autism or Asperger's Syndrome, and their Peers.* **Arlington, TX: Future Horizons.**

This new edition of *The Social Story Book* comes 20 years after Social Stories™ were introduced to help children with ASD learn social skills and better understand the world around them.

Savner, Jenifer L. and Smith Myles, Brenda (2000) *Making Visual Supports Work in the Home and Community: Strategies for Individuals with Autism and Asperger Syndrome.* **Shawnee Mission, KS: AAPC Autism Asperger Publishing Company.**

This book is very helpful in demonstrating the creation and use of visual strategies to help people with ASD across many setting, in school, home, community and work situations. This is an exceptional resource on visual strategies and how to implement them.

Books for Parents and Caregivers

Forrester-Jones, Rachel and Broadhurst, Sarah (2007) *Autism and Loss.* **London: Jessica Kingsley Publishers.**

This book is written to help caregivers understand how a person can be supported through all kinds of losses including bereavement, loss of friends, teachers, staff or possessions. Rachel Forrester-Jones helps caregivers learn to have the understanding, the skills and appropriate resources to work through many varied emotional reactions with the people they support. The book includes factsheets, and practical tools, worksheets, and exercises.

Smith, Harold Ivan (2012) *When a Child You Love is Grieving.* **Kansas City, MO: Beacon Hill Press.**

This book is full of compassionate ways to support a child who is grieving and underscores the necessity for a child to be able to grieve for as long as he or she needs to.

Smith, Harold Ivan, Johnson, Joy and Sieff, Janet (2007) *What Does that Mean?* **Omaha, NE: Centering Corporation.**

If a child is asking difficult questions about death and dying, this book helps to explain a myriad of terms related to death and dying.

Zucker, Robert (2009) *The Journey Through Grief and Loss Helping Yourself and Your Child When Grief is Shared.* **New York: St. Martin's Griffin.**

Rob Zucker's book is very helpful for parents of all kids and teens when they are all suffering from the pain of losing a loved one. He explains differences in the ways that children and adults may grieve, explains what to do when grief becomes complicated, and includes wonderful resources.

Journaling and Art Space

Feel free to use this space to draw, write, paint, collage, paste, tape or glue anything you like in these pages. This space can be used for whatever creative activities you choose.